D1557311

CZECHOSLOVAKIA:

The Bureaucratic Economy

Ota Šik

CZECHOSLOVAKIA:
The Bureaucratic Economy

International Arts and Sciences Press, Inc., White Plains, N.Y.

Library of Congress Catalog Card Number: 74-183253

International Standard Book Number: 0-87332-003-4

©1972 by International Arts and Sciences Press, Inc.
901 North Broadway, White Plains, New York 10603

Printed in the United States of America

Great Nations are never impoverished
by private, though they sometimes are
by public prodigality and misconduct.

—Adam Smith

CONTENTS

INTRODUCTION TO AMERICAN EDITION   3

INTRODUCTION TO GERMAN EDITION   25

Chapter 1
HOW WE HAVE BUILT UP OUR ECONOMY   41

Chapter 2
HOW WE PRODUCE   55

Chapter 3
HOW WE CONDUCT OUR TRADE   71

Chapter 4
HOW WE LIVE   83

Chapter 5
HOW WE MANAGE OUR ECONOMIC LIFE   99

Chapter 6
OUR PROSPECTS   113

NOTES   129

INDEX   135

INTRODUCTION
TO AMERICAN EDITION

INTRODUCTION
TO AMERICAN EDITION

The television talks which constitute the main content of this book were delivered in late June and early July 1968. Barely had the series been completed when Soviet tanks came thundering into the streets of Prague. Publication in book form had to be scrapped, and it was not until 1969 that a German edition was published. The introduction to that edition still contains much that is relevant and therefore it has been retained in the present book. However, this book is not merely about things past, but also about processes presently reappearing in Czechoslovakia's economic life. Its publication offers me a welcome opportunity to give the American reader some insight into the situation in my country today.

I have endeavored to demonstrate in practical terms the pass to which Czechoslovakia has been brought by twenty years under the Soviet-type economic system, for by 1951 the final touch had been applied to that process which, initiated in 1948, left her people with an economic system that took scant note of realities.

That the centralized, command system of planning practiced in the Soviet Union was wholly unsuited to an industrially advanced country, one, moreover, which relied very considerably on trade with the industrialized economies of the West, was obvious from the outset to those Marxist economists whose views were beginning to carry weight in the years immediately following World War II. These men were also aware that the Soviet methods of planning and management were products of Russia's economic backwardness, of her need to industrialize, and of the simple, unsophisticated structure of the production relations underlying the process. They were aware of the folly of copying a system that had abolished the market relationships among industrial concerns and, on the contrary, they realized that the change-over to socialism in their country necessitated a planned harnessing of the market mechanism in the public interest.

But on orders from Moscow, these Marxist economists — in common with many respected non-Marxist economists and politicians before them — were cast out into the political wilderness, and not a few paid with their lives. The show trials of the 1950s served in Czechoslovakia (as in the other "People's Democracies" of the day) to stamp out any independent thinking on economic and political matters and to ensure that only those willing to toe the Moscow line would be allowed a say in running the country. These preliminaries cleared the way for adapting all branches of the Czechoslovak economy to the Soviet model.

The product was a monolithic monopoly that left neither freedom of operation to producers nor freedom of choice to the buyer. The vast bureaucratic apparatus that emerged from this system set out to plan all industry, to apportion plant and manpower to the enterprises, to fix all prices at the stroke of a pen (for some $1\frac{1}{2}$ million lines of goods), to decide all aspects of foreign trade, and so on. Ensconced in their splendid isolation, totally indifferent to whether industries showed profits or losses, the bureaucrats supervised all the processes of production and distribution. Since they were in no position to judge the quality of the goods turned out, and were incapable of mastering the mass of complicated interrelationships in an industrial economy, they resorted to handing down plans for huge aggregates of products in terms of quantity, leaving the enterprises to make the detailed decisions about how to do the job within that framework.

But the enterprises, lacking all the previous criteria upon which to base their decisions, were now subjected to pressures of a different nature. Sales, for instance, were no longer of any interest since everything they produced under the plan was automatically distributed among the buyers. Earnings were no longer determined by sales, but by plan fulfillment and the corresponding financial handouts from the central authorities. Even production costs were now a matter of indifference since there were no competitors in the field, and the new officialdom was incapable of judging such things in practical terms. As for the customer, deprived of the opportunity to shop elsewhere, he could no longer influence quality or product lines (the microstructure of production), and simply had to take what was offered.

In the course of this book I have described in some detail the effect of all this on enterprise performance. It soon became clear that the plan was not a feasible substitute for market criteria and stimuli, that once market prices, competitive pressure, the freedom to shop around, and earnings tied to success on the market were done away with, industrial output no longer catered to the needs of the community. It was hardly a difficult problem for firms to fulfill the overall targets for growth in output, but they did so increasingly at the expense of economic operation, of quality, technological progress, and a rational industrial structure. Neither the individual managers, nor the enterprises as such, were at fault — it was all a result of the entirely new conditions under which they had to operate. And for the people of Czechoslovakia the consequences were little short of disastrous.

Disastrous does not, of course, signify complete and utter collapse — it takes more than a few decades to reduce the economy of a country to ruin. With natural resources available and with people working, goods will be produced and consumed. For years, indeed for decades, consumption can actually rise, for instance at the price of underinvestment in areas that can be overlooked for a time — such matters as maintenance of housing, repair and construction of roads, railroads and other forms of transportation, communications, the retail network, construction of apartments, schools and hospitals. And countries (such as the USSR) favored with immense natural resources can maintain production growth for a while by constantly expanding industrial capacity and employing more and more manpower, and this despite a piling up of the defects described above.

Such defects as an industrial microstructure out of line with the structure of needs, slow technological progress, and excessive inputs of materials, labor, and capital investment will retard advances in productivity, per-capita consumption and overall growth in national income, but retarding does not mean bringing things to a halt. Consumption may grow slowly, or stagnate, according to the magnitude of the defects in the particular economy and the extent of the natural resources on which the given country can draw. But the fact is that all the "socialist" countries are lagging more and more behind the industrially advanced countries of the West as regards productivity, national income and per-capita consumption, and the pages that follow provide ample evidence of this with respect to Czechoslovakia. And where growth of per-capita national income lags, not even a socialist system of distribution can help close the gap in consumption levels compared with the industrialized capitalist countries.

In the "socialist" world, of course, these things are carefully concealed. And since, in their anxiety to demonstrate the "superiority" of socialism over capitalism, the rulers maintain a firm hold and exercise strict censorship over the social sciences and statistics, critical analysis and exposure of the appalling economic problems are effectively blocked. Czechoslovakia has been exceptional in that a moment came when it was possible to make a fairly detailed examination of the economy and to embark on some important comparative studies. Fortunately, I was able to draw on these when preparing the talks published in this volume. The studies and the state of affairs they revealed, together with the scheme for a new economic model which Czechoslovak economists had elaborated, contributed

in no small measure to the movement that led to the ousting, in
January 1968, of Novotný's bureaucratic regime.

It seemed then that the years which scholars in Czechoslovakia had devoted to all-round theoretical spadework might
bear fruit, that an entirely new, democratic type of socialism
might be brought into being. But the military intervention of
August 1968 put an end to these hopes. That brutal and shortsighted act was motivated by fear — fear on the part of the
rulers of the neighboring "socialist" countries that the Czechoslovak infection might spread to their own people, and fear
among the incompetent hard-line political bosses in Czechoslovakia that reform of the system would sweep them from office.
The prime aim in sending in the tanks was to stop the reform.
As ideological justification for the act it was claimed that there
had been a danger of "antisocialist counterrevolution," although
none of the reformers, nor any other political group of any significance, had even so much as dreamed of a return to capitalism. Forces in the country capable of turning back the clock in
that way simply did not exist. What did exist was an unprecedented nationwide enthusiasm for the idea of a democratic, hu-
mane reform of socialist society. But the enthusiasm and the
hopes were crushed beneath the treads of the Soviet tanks.

The regime of Alexander Dubček, who had embarked on the
reform program after the downfall of Novotný in January 1968,
fell victim to the Soviet occupation. His brief term of office
ended in the spring of 1969 when, on the insistence of the masters in Moscow, Gustav Husák took his place. Step by step,
against the will of the overwhelming majority of the people, but
backed by the tremendous show of military might, Husák has
dismantled all the reform measures. He has put the economy,
and all other areas of public life, back to where they were under Novotný; he has reinstated the old centralized, command
system of planning, dissolved the workers' councils (self-
management in industry), tightened the government monopoly
of foreign trade and the monopoly type of industrial organization, cancelled all measures designed to create market prices,
and so on. To crown it all he has restored the Communist

Party, the sole political organization in the country, to its pre-vious status of supreme arbiter over the economy and the rest of public life.

Officially this reinstatement of the Stalinist model is de-scribed as "normalization" and "consolidation."

Now, as I write this introduction, the first "elections" to be held since the Soviet invasion are about to take place. They are de-signed to climax the "consolidation" phase. There is a remark-able similarity between the current election propaganda and that put out during the Novotný era. Lacking a built-in mecha-nism to ensure that production will grow and turn out the re-quired goods, the leaders of the "socialist" countries always fall back on resounding appeals, "mobilizing" the people for re-doubled efforts on the labor front. So that Husák, as was the case with Novotný, is driven by the logic of his centralized sys-tem to counter its economic impotence by the same outworn phrases.

In 1954 Novotný promised:

"Our Communist Party, the leading force in the National Front, has but a single aim — to build up our socialist home-land and thereby to ensure happiness and satisfaction for the working people. But this is impossible without hard, deter-mined work, without tackling our shortcomings, our errors and many obstacles. Nor is it possible without fighting the class enemies who are out to thwart the efforts of the working people.

"The aim of our entire economic effort is to raise the living standard of the working people. The aim of capitalist econo-mies is to increase profits, that is, to impoverish the workers. So you see that despite all shortcomings, which we do not deny, and we speak frankly to you about them, our economic system rests on sound foundations and the course we have taken to de-velop it is correct." (1)

So the people labored, they battled against the shortcomings, and the regime hunted down the class enemies (where enemies were lacking, they were fabricated). Yet the shortcomings did not diminish, and the leaders — to their sorrow — were com-pelled again and again to acknowledge them and to respond to the mounting protests from the working people. Some ten years later, in 1963, Novotný was again confessing:

"...Over the past years we have undoubtedly achieved many positive things which predominate in the development of our society, but we have also experienced mistakes and shortcomings...." (2)

"Yesterday, at a meeting of the Central Committee Secretariat, we discussed a report from the Party Control Commission concerning letters received from working people. There are signed and unsigned letters...in them people point to the shortcomings they have encountered. Many of the correspondents have been unable to get attention for their views and proposals, and so they write letters." (3)

The battle against shortcomings went on, but there could be no change in the system dictated by Moscow. Consequently, by 1967 the labors of the Czech and Slovak working people had resulted in a standard of living more than 50 percent lower than that obtaining in West Germany.

Now, in 1971, we have Gustav Husák repeating — in almost identical terms — the promises made by Novotný in 1954 and 1963.

"We have a program of social, legal, personal and state security, a program of peaceful creative work and life for millions of people, a program for the progressive development of our society.

"And further...just as we have a program in other sectors, in the sphere of raising living standards we shall, during these five years, tackle step by step the urgent problems of the working people or improve measures already taken. Naturally, the precondition is that we develop working initiative.

"...Capitalist society has always been concerned to conceal the shortcomings, to prevent the millions of working people from seeing through the regime of exploitation imposed by the ruling class. We have no such concern. We have but a single aim: to eliminate shortcomings and bungling wherever they occur and to correct mistakes....

"And of these we have no scarcity; there is slackness,

bungling, all too many things that need correcting and eliminating. People write to us from all over the Republic: 'You at the top,' they write, 'maybe you mean well and make eloquent speeches, but you should come and have a look at our village, at our town.' And they specify the things that are wrong in their areas." (4)

The very things that people were complaining about twenty years ago, and which Novotný had criticized and promised to put right in almost every speech, are today acknowledged by Husák. Anxious though he is to be as different as possible from his predecessor, Husák has no choice but to make the same appeals — but, unfortunately for him, he is making them after the Prague Spring. The years of the pre-Spring experience and the revelations made during it opened people's eyes to the impossibility of correcting the all-too-familiar shortcomings under the existing system, since they are implicit in the whole setup. With a public awareness totally different from that of the pre-Spring days, the efforts of the Husák regime stand revealed as something more than the old quixotic exercise; they are outright hypocrisy.

Naturally, most of the present leaders realized long ago that the centralized command planning was incapable of keeping the economy on a sound and balanced course that ensured growth of per-capita national income on a par with, for example, the market economies of the West. They know perfectly well that people cannot, just by working harder, prevent obsolescence of the technical base and make up for inadequate material and technical inputs to industry, for losses stemming from the structural imbalance between supply and demand, or for resources sunk in unfinished construction projects which take longer and longer to complete. The same is true for losses sustained in foreign trade operations, where prices are steadily moving to the disadvantage of Czechoslovak exports and imports. With the best will in the world the people in the factories cannot alter these economic processes, because as individuals and as working groups they are forced by objective processes completely beyond their control to act in a way which inevitably

creates new problems for other groups and enterprises; and
so it goes on.

The fact that the behavior of industrial groups is inescapably
governed by these objective conditions was shown long ago by
economic studies in Czechoslovakia. The situation is beyond
the control of even the best managers, planners and government departments. Involving, as it does, such a multitude of
contradictory processes, no planning mechanism, even with the
aid of the most sophisticated computers, can possibly function
successfully. It has been demonstrated that, despite its deficiencies, the market mechanism is the sole medium capable of
dealing with the complex interrelationships in a modern industrial economy. Socialism, far from trying to abolish the market relationships, should strive to improve them, to overcome
the defects of monopoly, to provide indirect state regulation by
means of macroeconomic planning designed to ensure that the
market moves in harmony with the long-term aims of society.

Toward the end of the Novotný regime, Husák was an enthusiastic advocate of the economic reform which, based on the
foregoing analyses, aimed at securing the planned regulation of
the market mechanism. While economics was a closed book to
Husák, he regarded the reform movement — which increasingly
was taking the shape of a political fight against Novotný — as
an effective means of toppling his enemy and of getting a foothold on the political ladder. Hence, in supporting the reform
proposals he was active in giving a radical political content to
the campaign.

But with Novotný ousted and Husák installed in high office, it
immediately became obvious that the radical campaigner had
utterly failed to grasp the need for thorough reform as a cure
for the ills of the economy. He no longer even tried to understand that without market pressures, and without awakening interest among enterprises in the market, the necessary structural and technological changes could not be brought about. Nor
did he grasp that there could be no progress without a determined dismantling of the bureaucratic apparatus, freeing the
enterprises from command planning and giving them economic

independence through self-management. Husák suddenly
emerged as a Stalinist advocate of economic centralism, whose
sole aim had been to get rid of his rival, Novotný. Shortly after
assuming office he began to invoke the arguments of the planning authority against the reformers.

From the moment when our draft proposals received official
sanction in 1965, that is, when Novotný was still in power, the
planning authority and other government departments had
launched an astute antireform campaign. Clearly, any serious
move to implement the new ideas would make the uselessness
of their mammoth apparatus painfully evident. Yet forthright
opposition to reform was, at the time, a nonstarter. Consequently, the wily guardians of the old order had recourse to the
inconspicuous tactic of procrastination. This was easy enough,
since the Novotný men had relegated implementation of the reform to the bureaucratic apparatus. Meanwhile, the planners
elaborated a line of argument which ran roughly as follows:

"While the reform model for a socialist market economy is
fundamentally correct, it can be no more than a long-term aim.
Given the present economic disequilibrium, it is impracticable.
The first thing to do is effect structural changes in a planned
way, restore the market balance; thereafter it should be possible to give the enterprises independence and to establish market relations. The only way to regain balance is by planned adjustment of the investment structure, by controlled price increases for consumer goods and services to provide funds for
bigger capital investment. Theoretically the reformers are
right, but their ideas are abstract and they are out of touch
with the economic realities."

Simultaneously with these devious arguments, the Planning
Office took the practical step of urging higher capital expenditures and prices with a view to safeguarding investment
schemes, at the price, of course, of lowering living standards.
The idea here, in addition to clinging to the increasingly difficult policy of extensive investment, was to discredit the reform
project.

The reformers, however, resolutely countered this dangerous

demagogy, pointing out in lectures, in the press, and in public debates the hypocrisy of the planners' measures and their supporting arguments. This was a fight against "controlled inflation" both in theory and in practice.* The public had to be helped to understand that the economic imbalance was not the product of a too rapid growth in personal consumption but, on the contrary, that its source lay in the overextended program of capital construction, with investment channeled into the wrong industries and technologically obsolete projects. The economic imbalance was a product of centralized planning that ignored the effectiveness of investment. With this type of investment program, it became increasingly difficult to provide the goods and services necessary to satisfy the purchasing power of wage earners; the "planned" development was, in fact, realized at the expense of the consumer.

What was required was not a stepping up of investment, but rather a relative decrease (in its share of national income), while ensuring intensified pressure on the producers; with the straitjacket of central command removed, the producers would be able to improve quality and proceed with technical innovation, to respond more flexibly to market demand and, by relying on the factors of production in their enterprises, to operate more economically. In short, with a relatively smaller volume of investment, there would be better performance and more effective growth.

The reformers elaborated a program for gradually dismantling the central command apparatus, and also for gradually introducing market prices and competitive pressures — for letting firms feel the influence of world prices. They were well

---

*A grotesque feature is that economic spokesmen in Prague are constantly depicting me as an advocate of "controlled inflation," although my opposition to this brainchild of the Planning Office is public knowledge. In point of fact, my intervention at a meeting of the Communist Party's Central Committee on May 3, 1967, denouncing moves of this nature, is a matter of record.

aware that the country's industry could not be exposed to market pressure at one stroke; a carefully planned transitional phase was essential — some five to seven years were envisaged (with the backing of substantial foreign credits, cooperation, purchase of licenses, etc.).

The planners, however, were never able to give a straight answer when the reformers asked them how they expected to achieve effective structural changes in investment and production when, with their arbitrarily fixed prices, there were no criteria whatever for judging the effectiveness of investment and when, moreover, the enterprises not only had no say but were, in fact, operating in a situation where the planning criteria actually bred antistimuli to any structural flexibility and technical progress.

Both before and after Novotný's fall, the arguments of the planners were welcomed by those political leaders who had a stake in preserving the centralized command system and its accompanying political administration. The duel fought during the Prague Spring between the reformers and the planning machine, while ostensibly concerned with the manner of implementing the economic reform, was, in essence, about abolishing or maintaining the Stalinist economic setup. As it proceeded there was some shifting of positions in the political arena. Quite a few people in the anti-Novotný camp, motivated by purely careerist considerations and with no serious desire to change the Stalinist system, began to shy clear of the reformers once the big boss had been toppled. They tried — usually on the quiet, in the lobbies, the ministries, the Party Presidium, and so on — to block the reform measures. In view of the powerful and growing public support for reform, however, they had to tread warily. The reformers, determined to nip these intrigues in the bud, coined the slogan: "No closed-door politics."

Husák, too, was anxious to preserve his image as a reformer, an image created during his fight against Novotný. But within the government he opposed every progressive move. While the reform economists were pressing for more independence for the enterprises, for cutting the volume of planned investment,

for anti-inflationary and antimonopoly measures, the Planning
Office and other ministries insisted on investment being stepped
up, enterprise independence curtailed, prices of consumer
goods and services raised. This antireform line was supported
by Husák, although he was always protesting that he was a nov-
ice in economics. Reinforced central planning, however, fitted
in with his Stalinist way of thinking, which not even his years
in prison had changed. He believed that, on the whole, the old
system was perfectly sound, that all that was needed was to put
a better man in the place of the incompetent Novotný, and evidently he had always seen himself in that role.

The moment the tanks and troops overran the country, Husák
and his associates realized that their day had come. Husák had
the advantage over the discredited Novotný Stalinists of being
a kind of new broom among politicians with, moreover, the reputation (especially in Slovakia) of having been a Novotný victim,
and of wearing the halo of a reformer. A man with such a reputation was infinitely more useful to the invaders than any of
the notorious and hated "collaborators." True, Husák had to
sing for the confidence reposed in him by the Soviets, and he
did so by making all the personnel changes they demanded and
by rescinding all reform measures. Understandably, the Soviets also "insured" themselves by surrounding Husák with
true-blue Stalinists in the seats of power. Once they had com-
plied by making these changes and by reinforcing the centralized system, it was safe to let Husák, Svoboda and similar figures enjoy the credit for having "prevented" Stalinist trials and
wholesale terror. The Security Service had diligently conjured
up the specter of these horrors, but in reality the Soviets had
no desire to raise the temperature on the international arena
by holding show trials; they were more concerned to dampen
the excitement about Czechoslovakia as quickly as possible. In
this, too, Husák could be much more useful to them than the
discredited Bilak, Indra, and others of their kind.

By opting for this course Husák had assumed the mantle of
Novotný, and whatever his intentions may be, the logic of the
old system drives him to rule in much the same manner as his

ill-starred predecessor, whom he personally loathes and de-
tests. Like Novotný before him, he has had to embark on per-
secuting those — communists and noncommunists — who are
not to the liking of his Kremlin masters and who are classified
as "unreliable" or "hostile" elements. Just as in the past, an
"antisocialist counterrevolutionary conspiracy" was invented,
and orders went out to remove all incriminated persons from
political posts and to mete out exemplary punishment to them.
Once again the axe of victimization has fallen on men and wom-
en who, by advocating a form of socialism more suited to
Czechoslovak conditions and by stressing that there are more
ways than one of pursuing the socialist goal, failed to comply
with the Kremlin's concept of "socialism" and refused to rec-
ognize Soviet hegemony.

True, the sentences now being imposed are mild compared
with the wholesale executions and life imprisonments of the
1950s, but show trials have been so discredited that nowadays
communist regimes are shy of repeating them. They have not,
however, renounced lesser political trials as a weapon against
recalcitrant citizens. Even under Husák the number of convictions for political offenses in various parts of the country has
reached several hundred. Tens of thousands have been victim-
ized, left to scrape for a living as best they can, and are often
hounded from job to job.

Indeed, there is really little difference between the persecu-
tion of yesterday and that of today: while the sentences were
horrifying, the underlying purpose, then as now, was to get rid
of men who were not acceptable to the Russians and replace
them with reliable yes-men. Actually, the number of people
persecuted in Czechoslovakia today is greater than in the 1950s.
Yet Husák seems to think he is using kid-glove methods, and in
the above-quoted speech he seeks to justify this, while also con-
veying a threat against those who refuse to submit to his regime, and hence to the Soviet dictate. (5)

Anyone who at any time, in any area within the Soviet sphere,
has deviated ever so slightly from the straight and narrow path
of Soviet intentions has had, sooner or later, to reckon with

political disgrace and punishment. It is an irony of fate that Husák, who at one time fell into disfavor due to quite insignificant attempts to adapt Party policy in Slovakia to the specific conditions of that nation, and was ruthlessly punished, now appears in the role of the hatchet man compelled to bear false witness in the identical terms and to persecute those who have tried to adapt the form of socialism to the conditions of an economically and culturally advanced country and to its progressive democratic traditions.

In 1954, after much suffering and on utterly false charges, Husák was condemned to life imprisonment for "attempting to destroy the independence and unity of the Republic...." Addressing the 10th Congress of the Czechoslovak Communist Party in 1954, Antonín Novotný said: "The lengths to which these bourgeois nationalist agents are ready to go has been demonstrated at the recent trial in Bratislava of the Husák group. These bourgeois nationalists have been unmasked as the worst enemies of the Republic; they have caused untold harm both in the economy and in other sectors. They sought to conceal their real purpose — return to the old capitalist order — under nationalistic slogans. Their purpose was to destroy the Republic, to set the fraternal nations of Czechs and Slovaks against each other, and to sow enmity among the other nationalities in Slovakia against the Slovak nation so that the bourgeoisie might take advantage of the disunity." (6)

In 1971, Husák, referring to people he knows quite well never wanted a return to capitalism and whose sole aim was to make socialism more attractive and viable, declared that they "wanted to subvert our society, to tear it away from the socialist camp." In labeling these people as counterrevolutionaries he is responding to the same pressures that brought about his own condemnation as a counterrevolutionary. He has let loose, and allowed others to let loose, the same wave of anti-Semitism that accompanied the Slánský trial in 1952 and, to an even greater degree, the "bourgeois nationalist" trials of 1954. Once again we find people being accused of collusion with international Zionist organizations and their allegedly "anticommunist

activities in Czechoslovakia," although Husák fully realizes
that this is playing down to the basest passions, that it is in the
pattern of the fascist thugs.

It is the way of the world that anyone who undertakes to serve
masters who invoke "socialism" purely as a window dressing
for their power game is bound to serve them to the end. So
long as he pursues policies that conform to alien interests he
will be sure of an "attractive" job, but should he be out of step
just once, he can be certain that his number will be up.

In the speech that we just quoted Husák thunders, as Novotný
did so often before him, "Those who fail to come up to the mark
in their work or their moral qualities cannot hold responsible
positions in a socialist society." Naturally, he is not thinking
of himself.

What opportunity have the people of Czechoslovakia ever had
to influence the choice of men for leading posts? None whatever! This has always been the preserve of the Party machine,
a means of maintaining its grip on all spheres of life. From
top to bottom, from national all the way down to local levels,
the machine sees to the placing of reliable and obedient instruments of Party policy, men on whom, moreover, its officials
throughout the country can rely for personal support.

This building of a power base through appointing the right
men has always been the "art of arts" for Party bosses, on
which their careers and their fate in the political infighting depend. And the same is true for the staffing of the economic machine and all other sectors of public life. Reliability in this
sense is a far better recommendation than any considerations
of skill or moral qualities. It is common knowledge that all in-
vitations to the public to say what they think about the qualities
of leading officials are mere propaganda gestures. The workers' councils, which in 1968 gave people in Czechoslovakia
their first opportunity to have a real say in choosing and controlling managers, were later banned for the very reason that
they constituted a serious threat to the manipulatory role of
the Party machine.

As in the economic sphere, so in the political, and even more

so if that is possible. Elections are a farce designed to create
the impression of public support. True, the world has by now
seen through the carefully staged formality enacted around the
ballot box — but then it is in the nature of a bureaucratic regime to present formalities as the essence of a process while
the essential qualities are ignored and suppressed. The formal
act of "election" is presented as the height of democracy, while
genuine freedom to elect representatives, freedom of political
assembly, freedom of the spoken and printed word, these are
brushed aside as mere "bourgeois formalities."

Under the communist system candidates for "election" are
handpicked by the Party machine from among those members,
and a few nonmembers, who can be relied on to obey it in all
things. Candidate lists are submitted to the electorate via the
National Front. Election day is a formal demonstration, with
participation carefully controlled by Party agents in all areas.
Officials at the polling stations are selected from among trained
members of the Party machine, security officers, and so on —
an array of people capable of ensuring both the necessary pressure on voters and, should there still be rather too many dis-
senting votes or spoiled ballots, the appropriate adjustment of
the results.

By the time this book appears in America the elections in
Czechoslovakia will be over. The regime will have celebrated
its victory, a victory decided beforehand. And this will not be
simply a propaganda exercise for the benefit of the public at
home and abroad; the bureaucratic regime will also have per-
suaded itself that the elections really demonstrated support
among a majority of the population.

To the Western reader it must seem incomprehensible that
serious politicians can time after time go through the motions
of approving such campaigns and regard them as achievements
of "political activity." What the public thinks on such occasions
is beside the point. It is of no importance whether people actually participate in the meetings, assemblies and elections, or
whether the events are packed by a bunch of Party hacks, by
people pressured into attendance or transported from place to

place by shock workers. What matters is that an event has taken place, it has been duly recorded in the appropriate offices, and "political activity" has been demonstrated.

While the motions of political campaigning are performed, those in the seats of power live their own lives, absorbed in their own struggle. And the ordinary people live their own, separate lives, far removed from the political and public arena, indifferent to public events, insulated to the maximum degree from all that. The depth of the alienation of labor, industry, administration, and state power has never been equalled by any capitalist society. In this form of alienation we have a concentrated expression of the fact that the communist regimes have nothing in common with socialism. They are state-capitalist systems in which the working people are governed, repressed, and exploited by a power elite relying on a Party and state bureaucracy of unprecedented proportions.

With the labor force thus alienated from the production process, from the means of production, from the fruits of labor, from the management of industrial enterprises, from the plan and so on, economic problems are vastly multiplied. There is no enthusiasm; "socialist emulation" and the like are ritual exercises organized by Party and trade union officials. The workers do no more and no better than is required by the level of supervision. Shoddy work produces ever-increasing numbers of rejects; absenteeism and pilfering are on the increase. Many workers, especially the skilled craftsmen, supplement their earnings by doing odd jobs "on the side" for private individuals. Their services are much in demand due to the shortage of repair shops and other facilities resulting from the lagging of the tertiary sector.

The steady decline in working morale cannot be stemmed by political speeches, "moral" appeals, or Party controls. It is an expression of the deep-seated alienation of the people from economic and public life in all the "socialist" countries and, understandably, it is most pronounced in Czechoslovakia, where there is an added element of protest and resistance against foreign military intervention, the occupation by Soviet troops and the suppression of the reform movement. The huge economic losses caused by bureaucratic planning and management, which the workers observe at first hand, serve but to aggravate the demoralization.

Although, with a view to placating the public, the Husák regime has been trying to boost imports and domestic production of consumer goods, it has had to do so at the expense of reducing investment. But the decline in capital expenditures is not accompanied by intensified market pressure on the producers and a consequent improvement in the quality and effectiveness of investment, as the reformers envisaged, and is simply a structural adjustment of the state plan. Therefore the planned cut will be felt in coming years in the form of deficiencies in the production base, with a growing obsolescence and lag behind the Western countries.

The regime is silent about the economic ills. They are not permitted to be statistically followed and recorded; economic analyses, insofar as they are made, are not for public view. The progressive economists have been "purged." The hopeful progress of recent years in economic studies has been halted; in the research institutes and university departments we see a revival of the old Stalinist scholasticism, which has nothing in common with serious scientific study and serves solely to camouflage the existing practices.

And so we find today a return to the type of economic practice depicted in our analysis of the Novotný regime in the present book. Consequently, the talks delivered in 1968 are of more than historical interest, for they present to the American reader most of the features of the contemporary communist economies. Although, naturally, there are differences when it comes to practical matters, by and large it can be said that in all these countries there is the same type of purposeless and uneconomic activity in investment, production and trade, and management, with broadly the same effects on the standard of living.

One can only hope for the day when the nations in this part of the world, and the people of Czechoslovakia among them, will

throw off the repressive regimes masquerading under "socialist" catchwords and be able to go forward in freedom. Although
we do not know when that moment will come, come it must because, in human history, every regime that has stood in the
way of economic and cultural advance and has maintained its
grip solely by ideological brainwashing, censorship, political
oppression, in short by wielding power against the people, has
sooner or later been swept away by the people.

Ota Šik
Basel, September 1971

INTRODUCTION
TO GERMAN EDITION

INTRODUCTION
TO GERMAN EDITION*

This survey of the state of the Czechoslovak economy was delivered verbatim in a series of television talks shortly before the occupation of the country. I have intentionally refrained from making any subsequent alterations in the script. The facts it presents came as a shock to many people in Czechoslovakia because, under Novotný's rule, they had never been able to see the whole situation. Although the true state of affairs had been familiar to economists for a long time, the political regime could not risk the danger of public knowledge.

In view of their strong impact on the thinking and attitude of our citizens, the talks acquired no small economic and political significance. Despite the shock of learning the facts after years of rose-tinted propaganda, the response was not one of depression and pessimism; on the contrary, when the initial surprise was over, there was a great determination and a truly enthusiastic endeavor to eliminate the root causes of the shortcomings.

True, for years people had been observing the contrast between official propaganda, with its boasts about economic successes, and their own day-to-day experience, which told them something quite different. But while their faith in the propaganda was steadily waning, they could learn nothing about the actual overall state of the economy from their individual

---

*Fakten der tschechoslowakischen Wirtschaft, Wien-München-Zürich, Verlag Fritz Molden, 1969. The Introduction was written in Basel in November 1968.

encounters with the shortcomings. They had no opportunity to
test their observations on a wide scale, to make the necessary
generalizations and comparisons, to distinguish long-term
trends from short-term fluctuations, or to uncover the causes
and underlying connections among the general negative processes. In short, they had no chance to reinforce their personal experience with the essential economic theory and scientific
analysis.

The facts about the economy had to be revealed frankly
through the mass medium of television, not merely to provide
people with information, but also to enable them to understand
that various measures would have to be taken, at times involving some "unpopular" steps, if economic development was to
be changed and improvement in living standards was to be ac-
celerated. The truth was indeed alarming, and it revealed the
grave lag in development behind the economies of most Western European countries. The conservatives in our country and,
of course, first of all many politicians responsible for the past
policies, declared that the survey "blackened the entire socialist development." They insisted that I was intent on denying
the great successes of socialist progress.

There are orthodox Communists who interpret their mem-
bership in the movement as meaning that always and under all
circumstances one should demonstrate that a socialist economy
develops better than a capitalist economy. Should the facts
speak against this contention, one should, in their view, sup-
press or ignore such facts. They look upon any publication or
use of such facts as an antisocialist act. This point of view un-
derlies the whole campaign conducted against me, both by orthodox members of the Czechoslovak Communist Party and by
members of some other communist parties. By my public revelation of Czechoslovakia's economic lag behind capitalist
countries, I was allegedly pursuing antisocialist, counterrevolutionary aims.

Such a political viewpoint is quite obviously shortsighted and
disastrous. The facts can be concealed and obscured for a
time, but not forever. Czechoslovakia cannot be hermetically

sealed off from the rest of the world. Contacts with other countries enable comparisons to be made, and sooner or later the
truth starts to trickle through. Were it just a matter of short-
term, temporary retardation, it could, under certain circumstances, be passed over in silence. But it is impossible to conceal a long-term and, moreover, steadily widening gap. It is
certainly no accident that orthodox Communists have stopped
talking in recent years about catching up with and surpassing
the capitalist economies.

The longer the economy of the centralistic-bureaucratic system lags behind the capitalist economies in its development,
the greater will be the shock of awakening for the people of
Czechoslovakia. There is, indeed, a danger that their anger
might then turn against the very ideals of socialism and not
just against the false system of managing and leading the socialist system. Still more serious, however, is the fact that the
present centralistic-bureaucratic socialist systems are becom-
ing less and less attractive to the workers of capitalist countries, who can no longer be kept in the dark about their grave
defects.

Therefore, in revealing the true state of the economy of my
country, far from attacking its socialist essence, I am acting
in the conviction that we can overcome economic backwardness
while preserving our socialist forms of ownership. To state
the truth about a socialist economy is not an expression of hos-
tility to socialism; on the contrary, it speaks of a belief in the
untapped potentialities of socialism, a belief far more profound
than the convictions of those who are accusing me today of
counterrevolutionary intentions.

There is one way to save socialism: to make a radical change
in its economic and political model. In Czechoslovakia we were
trying, after January 1968, to set about making this change.
This meant that we had to convince the general public of the
need for such a step, and to win its support. The public had to
be shown how healthy economic progress could be achieved.
And the fact that people understood these things was proved by
their attitude: instead of giving in to depression on learning the

truth from my television talks, they showed a sound determination to make sacrifices if need be in order to change course.

For those who had founded their power on the old centralistic system, however, this truth was acutely dangerous. Like it or not, criticism of the shortcomings and backwardness of the Czechoslovak economy was immediately taken as a criticism of the centralistic-bureaucratic type of economic management predominating in most other socialist countries. It was a sudden revelation of the falsity of the propaganda that had kept people helpless for so long.

How indeed can the uninitiated judge whether an economy can develop otherwise than it has hitherto, whether supplies of goods and services could be better? The major problem is that an economy as a whole seldom experiences a long-term decline; usually it advances and there is overall growth, although with ups and downs. As long as there is even the most sluggish growth in production, the public is quite unable to judge whether progress could be more rapid, whether their consumption could increase more quickly, and so on. And here we have the basis for the entire pattern of biased and misleading propaganda.

First, publicity has been given solely to the rate of growth of production, while the trend of overall consumption and the extent to which people's real wants are satisfied have been omitted.

Second, the only yardstick used for assessing present levels is the level of the given country in the past (in Czechoslovakia, for instance, figures at the end of World War II or for the postwar years are taken; in the USSR, figures for tsarist Russia), and the economic development of other industrially advanced countries is left out of the picture.

As we shall show later, the growth rate of production tells us nothing about the overall movement of personal and social consumption, which orthodox Communists also regard as the true aim of production. Figures for rising output throw no light on the superfluous production for its own sake that offers no end effect for the population. They say nothing about the unnecessary waste, the unwanted products, or about goods consumed just for the lack of anything better or more useful.

Finally, the growth rate of production gives absolutely no indication of how production and consumption might advance if the industrial structure were correct, if technological progress were more rapid, if working morale were better, and if concern about improving quality were more intense.

Yet a rise in the volume of output, although the industrial structure and the quality of products may be unsuitable and entail unnecessary waste, is enough to give the layman the impression of success. Moreover, in certain countries and under certain conditions (a serious shortage of basic products, postwar development, the situation in developing countries, etc.), growth in the amount of output alone, providing some measure of advance in consumption, may afford a sense of satisfaction and can therefore be taken as the main yardstick of economic success. In this event, however, the fact that, with more economical operation or a better structural trend, consumption could rise more rapidly is intentionally overlooked.

But there comes a point when merely quantitative growth is not enough. For one thing, people are no longer satisfied with mounting supplies of more or less the same products, and they start to demand rapid changes in the types of goods, steadily improving quality, and wider assortments. What is more, growth in quantity is held back by slow progress in quality: failure to improve the quality of machinery and equipment as required, slow technological development, and stagnation in the industrial structure operate more and more as brakes on any advance in the volume of output. Under these circumstances, propaganda that persists in comparing merely the volume of current production with that in times long past becomes a means for concealing the basic weakness of the economy. People are not allowed to realize that the given volume of output could yield a much higher level of consumption if it were not for the unnecessary wastage, the stagnating quality, and the rigid industrial structure; that, indeed, a far slower growth rate could permit a much more rapid advance in the consumption of what is produced if production were to develop in a different way.

These are the potentialities revealed by thorough economic
analysis and by comparative studies that confront the trends of
production and consumption with the corresponding trends in
countries where the natural conditions are similar and the initial levels were the same or even worse. Such comparative
studies provided the groundwork for my television talks and,
of course, the chapters that follow. The outcome has been a
profound revelation of the untapped potentialities in the Czechoslovak economy, of the big losses incurred in public consumption and the growing lag of the living standard behind the level
reached by countries that had a worse start than Czechoslovakia after World War II. Our people's knowledge of these facts,
their determination to put an end to this state of affairs, com-
bined with a thorough overhaul of the system of economic management, could have laid the basis for achieving healthy development and far better results than hitherto. However, the occupation of our country by force has interrupted this promising
development.

The occupation was followed by a political campaign in the
press and elsewhere against anyone who had been working for
radical reform. I was accused of trying to turn our economy
back to capitalism, of carrying out measures at the expense of
the workers, of yearning for a bourgeois mode of life, and so
on.

These were, in fact, the old techniques of propaganda: employing the bald assertion, labeling without a shred of evidence,
without argument or analysis. The very method employed in
this propaganda suggests that the mainspring of the campaign
was the desire of political bosses to avoid uncomfortable criticism and to ward off the danger of having their managerial incompetence revealed, rather than an understanding of the "capitalist danger" to the Czechoslovak economy. There is nothing
easier, when acting from positions of power, than to label someone a counterrevolutionary because there is no need to offer
reasoned proof and all argument is ruled out by censorship.

Typical of this propaganda routine is an article by Dr. Ger-
hard Schulz in Neues Deutschland, of September 9, 1968, entitled

"Die untaugliche Konzeption Ota Šiks" [Ota Šik's Unworkable
Concept]. It is a classic example of how an entire mode of
argument and all contentions can be subordinated to a given
political aim — in this case, to wipe the floor ideologically with
Šik's concept, no matter whether the statements correspond to
the economic reality or whether they help or harm its development.

Professor Schulz evidently relies on the fact that the pages
of newspapers in the German Democratic Republic are not ac-
cessible to anyone wishing to answer him. He writes under the
protection of power at the top and under a fully centralized
press censorship. Consequently, he is free to say anything that
will serve to crush an opponent and, in response to "wishes
from on high," to transform him into a counterrevolutionary.
Whether on orders, or in an attempt to earn the highest praise,
the fact is that he is not the slightest bit concerned to provide
a truthful presentation of my views, or to reply to serious arguments founded on fact. After all, nothing more is needed than
the time-honored method of ascribing to one's opponent views
he has never held, taking sentences out of context, and then
dealing him a crushing blow. No proof is required; general
statements are sufficient.

The Professor shows no interest whatsoever in the abundance
of hard fact, both in my book Plan and Market Under Socialism
and in the television talks, concerning the lag of the Czechoslovak economy, the low productivity rate compared with Western
countries, the enormous and growing disproportions, and the
ineffective production for production's sake. He simply reiter-
ates that Czechoslovakia's output in 1958 was double the 1937
figure. He ignores the substantially slower growth in consumption, as compared with capitalist countries, that stems from
the abovementioned shortcomings in production. Such facts
have to be concealed from readers in his country.

Moreover, he completely distorts the principle of the economic model projected in Czechoslovakia by maintaining that
we were intent on introducing spontaneous movement of the
market, with a mechanism comparable to that of early capitalism. Anyone who acquaints himself with my book and with the

talks published in the present volume can see that, on the contrary, we were concerned with achieving an entirely novel synthesis between central macroeconomic planning and the market
mechanism. Indeed, we have always stressed that our aim is
not spontaneous, but centrally regulated, market operation.

Professor Schulz creates another bogey for the German
workers by insisting that the Czechoslovak revisionists were
out to build a system whereby enterprises would be threatened
by blind forces leading to bankruptcy, as under capitalism. No
one in Czechoslovakia has ever suggested such a thing.

True, a number of works were so obsolete, and their performance was so poor, that they were utterly incapable of achieving anything approaching the input-output levels or the quality
and production assortments common in the world. It is also
true that almost any type of production can be profitable under
the centralized-bureaucratic system. Administrative measures
are simply taken to fix prices high enough to cover all production costs. Then even the least productive and most inefficient
works can operate profitably. And Professor Schulz knows as
well as I do (or he should know) how prices are set by administrative measures — that they are always the outcome of negoti-
ations between enterprises and the central authorities, and that
the latter are ultimately incapable of refuting the figures presented by the enterprises. In the GDR, too, there must be a
good many enterprises that are able to show profits thanks
solely to prices set in this manner.

However, if such enterprises were forced to sell their products at world prices and to face the exacting demands of world
markets, many would be unable to compete. At world prices
they would not even cover their production costs, let alone make
a net profit. By protecting these concerns, allowing them relatively
high prices on the domestic market and not compelling them to
compete with sophisticated producers on the world market, or
by meeting their losses out of budget resources, the centralistic system keeps even the least economical and technologically
most backward producers in business. This, of course, is paid
for in terms of living standards; the more costly and inefficient

the performance of socialist enterprises as compared with firms in the West, the greater the discrepancy in the standard of living. Such are the ABC's of economics.

One is bound to ask what serves the public interest best: To protect backward enterprises, to keep them in glasshouse conditions, to present as an achievement of socialism the artificially created profitability derived from artificial prices that saves firms from liquidation at the expense of lower living standards for the working people? Or to provide strict conditions under which economic pressures will impel enterprises to match the performance of leading firms elsewhere, making them really get down to the job of closing the gap in productivity and production costs, and in the quality and structure of output, until they are capable of facing competitive markets? Naturally, in the latter case some enterprises will run into difficulties from time to time.

Those of us who were preparing the new model always emphasized, however, that some protection would have to be given for a while in cases where performance was held back by obstacles that could not be removed all at once (new plant going into operation, difficulty in procuring modern equipment, insuperable raw material problems, etc.). But there should be a clearly stated time limit; an enterprise should have a schedule for tackling its temporary difficulties, and it should know that sooner or later it will have to measure up to the more sophisticated producers.

Permanent state protection should be an exception, applying only to certain essential branches where domestic production cannot be replaced by imports and where, for various inescapable reasons, the producers are unable to compete with advanced standards. But when, instead of making it the exception, the centralistic-bureaucratic system protects almost all production, thereby markedly depressing the living standard of the entire community, this is certainly not meeting the wants of the workers or demonstrating the advantages of socialism. The general consensus of opinion among workers is undoubtedly in favor of a more rapid advance in living standards; to this end, they are in favor of enterprises being compelled by overall economic pressures to adapt constantly to leading world standards, or at least to the average type of production common in the advanced capitalist countries. Given even the most rigorous economic conditions, however, no one in Czechoslovakia has considered allowing enterprises to be threatened with bankruptcy, as Professor Schulz maintains. It would perhaps have been well if the Professor had made a serious study of our theoretical views before engaging in a polemic.

In the system we had elaborated, we envisaged a market regulated in a socialist manner. This included, among other features, overall prognosis at the center that could predict the effects of a given market situation in any of the large establishments (trusts or concerns). In that case the center would have to be informed in good time about economic difficulties occurring in an enterprise.

The question of physical liquidation arises in very few cases. In effect, we speak of liquidation in the economic sense, that is, liquidation of ineffective or unnecessary or utterly uncompetitive lines of production. That is something quite different from the physical liquidation of an enterprise.

When a firm is obliged to liquidate an unwanted line of production, it can always look for a substitute program that will meet market demands or offer an opportunity to compete. During the brief period in which our enterprises were subjected to stronger economic pressures, we saw how in some fields such progressive and radical changes in production programs can be implemented comparatively quickly.

Cases in which we envisaged the actual physical liquidation of an enterprise were exceptional (usually only single plants within larger establishments), and then only where such factors as antiquated buildings, the impossibility of changing unsuitable equipment, etc., ruled out any prospects of switching to new programs. Moreover, even in such cases there was no question of blind forces condemning firms to bankruptcy.

Where such a step is required, the central authorities or top managements responsible for the establishments concerned should know about it beforehand, and they should program the liquidation to ensure the best possible social conditions and to minimize the impact on the work force. (All this was discussed in the television talks.) Retraining facilities would have to be provided, with possible resettlement of superfluous labor and full compensation for any losses incurred by employees. In short, necessary structural and technological changes, benefiting the vast majority of the people, should be carried out on the condition that the working groups of the few establishments affected will suffer a minimum of material loss.

This puts our essential economic program, which was received with such remarkable understanding by the working people of our country, in quite a different light. In comparison, Professor Schulz's statements appear as obvious political demagogy. Like Mr. Novotný after January 1968, he has been declaring himself a guardian of the workers' interests and their social security against the attacks of "revisionist economists" who are out to "reinstate capitalist anarchy and spontaneity at the expense of the workers." How often history has shown that such "friends of the people" are merely political careerists, far more concerned with the ideological defense of certain reactionary political rulers than with the genuine interests of the working people!

It would perhaps be a more helpful contribution to a genuine polemic if these "friends of the people" in the German Democratic Republic and other centralistic-bureaucratic countries were to find the courage to adopt a serious approach and, as a beginning, publish my book Plan and Market Under Socialism, or these facts about the state of the Czechoslovak economy, in their countries. They would then be in a position to counter our views in factual terms and to do so openly before the public. They would save themselves a lot of work spent on finding quotations to fit their arguments.

If they took this approach they would probably find it difficult to assert, for example, that I require that production be corrected by the market after the event, without preliminary planned regulation of the underlying industrial structure, without applying scientific and technological findings in production, and without planning all phases of the reproduction process, including the market. Readers of my book would learn that, on the contrary, I am concerned with guiding all phases of reproduction (including the market) in a planned way, taking into account their dialectical interconnections. I have always maintained, however, that a central organ of society can predict the necessary industrial structure, the distribution of the national income, the structure of market demand, etc., only in terms of the most fundamental, overall proportions; that it cannot predict development in concrete detail and cannot avoid subjective errors in its plans and prognoses. And that is why the actual development of the market and the satisfaction in practice of the real needs of the population and society have to serve as an ever-present criterion and corrective of our plans, which are then seen as stemming from an unceasing act of planning that is continually gaining greater precision.

Thus, readers would realize that the model of a socialist synthesis between plan and market that we have been constructing over the years has been the product of a much more profound and lengthy process of analyzing the shortcomings of our economic development than anything the critics of the model have attempted. I am offering this comparative study for consideration by the public so that readers may decide for themselves where there has been an endeavor to discover objective truth and where there has been a transparent effort to conceal shortcomings.

I have taken the view, and I continue to hold it, that it is possible to overcome the grave shortcomings of the Czechoslovak economy without interfering with its socialist nature. But I am also convinced that substantial changes are imperative in the forms and methods of management and direction, and in the mechanisms by which the economy operates. Moreover, these changes must be given an institutional basis. Measures of this nature cannot be promoted and implemented if we fail to expose the defects and the backwardness of the existing system quite openly and uncompromisingly before the entire public. This alone is genuinely in the interests of the people, in contrast to all the abstract apologias extolling the present systems of planning and managing socialist economies, which merely serve to exonerate the people responsible for the unfortunate course of development.

CHAPTER 1

HOW WE HAVE BUILT UP OUR ECONOMY

HOW WE HAVE BUILT UP OUR ECONOMY

If we wish to understand the economic development of Czechoslovakia, and of many other socialist countries, we must acquaint ourselves at the outset with the two courses open to any country in the world, whether it is industrially advanced or at the threshold of its development, whether its system is socialist or capitalist. To put it briefly, an economy may develop extensively or intensively. A country aspiring to advance may concentrate on mobilizing new manpower reserves, on using its resources to install the maximum number of new machines, on building new factories, in which case it has adopted an extensive model of development; it may make greater use of existing capacities and manpower in the endeavor to raise its production level. In the latter case, of course, obsolescent machinery and techniques have to be replaced by more progressive types, the latest know-how has to be applied, organization must be improved, and management personnel must be kept up to the mark. Essentially this second, intensive, course meets the demands placed on an advanced economy by the scientific and technological revolution.

Naturally, we can never expect to find one unadulterated type of development in any country. The two alternatives always go hand in hand, with one or the other dominating. In the case of Czechoslovakia, the main trouble has been that it has pursued a predominantly extensive course, the prototype for which was the industrialization model sanctified in the Soviet Union by the personality of Stalin. And here we should add that when the extensive road is followed to an extreme it harbors the seeds of economic decline, and when the tolerable limit is passed this potential risk emerges as a reality, taking its inevitable toll in the shape of a decline in economic effectiveness, or even complete stagnation. As we know, this was what happened to the Czechoslovak economy in the early sixties. Before attempting to describe all the causes and effects we should perhaps try to deal with a question that will undoubtedly occur to the reader: Why, in fact, did an industrial country such as Czechoslovakia ever turn to the extensive type of development?

The reasons have to be sought in the first postwar years, when the Czechoslovak economy, and the economies of most European countries, were still crippled. Moreover, alongside the industrially advanced provinces of Bohemia and Moravia, the more backward Slovakia came into the postwar Republic. This factor alone made it imperative to plan for overall economic reconstruction and to include many new capacities in the program for expanding the industrial potential. And then, in the early fifties, the barriers of cold war that cut across Europe undoubtedly played their part. In those days a new element entered into Czechoslovakia's economic life — preparation for a possible "hot" war. Nor can we ignore the strong impact of oversimplified Stalinist economic views.

In tracing this trend, the Third Session of the Council for Mutual Economic Assistance (COMECON) stands out as a milestone. Czechoslovakia was criticized at this meeting because she was manufacturing light-industry products that relied on imported raw materials. For instance, there was talk of big wool imports and of an endeavor to produce woolen fabrics of English quality. For their part, however, the Czechoslovak economists saw the enormous opportunities offered by the empty shelves of Europe's shopkeepers.

It was also pointed out on this occasion that Czechoslovakia was not really lacking in her own raw materials. The contention was that buying abroad offered no special advantage and that an economy intent on expanding its own resources, even at the cost of heavy investment outlays, was far more stable. Inevitably, in the face of such criticism, Czechoslovakia was induced to choose an industrial program that would make her completely independent of foreign markets. Indeed, at this point her fellow members in COMECON expressly demanded that she curtail her contacts with the West and give her social- ist partners preference in all export trade. Of course, no one can have any doubt about the international duty of a socialist country, especially one as advanced as Czechoslovakia. On the other hand, one cannot quite overlook the fact that many coun- tries in the socialist camp, influenced as they were by Stalin's theories, lost their awareness of Czechoslovakia's specific needs.

The upshot was a planned withdrawal from many foreign markets to which Czechoslovakia will find it difficult to return, while development was switched over to the extensive model for good. This model, indissolubly linked as it was with Stalin's personality, was equated with socialism. Export trade with cap- italist countries, originally planned to reach 55 percent of total exports by 1953, was cut in the amended plan to 22 percent. The socialist countries were to take 78 percent of the trade instead of the envisaged 45 percent. Import trade underwent a similar change. (1)

In 1951 there was also a resetting of all targets for industrial branches. Output, which according to the original plan was to have risen by some 50 percent over the 1948 level by 1953 (157 percent), had to be nearly doubled (198 percent). Engineering output was to be almost trebled (291 percent), and the advance in heavy industry was to be more than twofold (233 percent). (2) Work was started on sinking new pits with a total capacity of 13 million tons of coal in the Ostrava, Most and Kladno basins, while the ore mines opened at this time did not offer promise of very great effectiveness. Construction of the New Klement Gottwald Iron and Steel Works at Kunčice was started, a project for a metallurgical complex at Košice was broached, and, among other proposals, there emerged a plan for fifteen ore-enriching plants.

We should mention in this connection that some outstanding Communist economists, among them Ludvik Frejka and Josef Frank, were victims of these drastic changes in economic policy. The indictment brought against them revolved, in effect, around the search for a specific Czechoslovak road to socialism. They were accused by the prosecution of not including extraction of ferrous and nonferrous ores in the economic plan, of closing down outdated works "under the pretext of reconstruction," of trying to preserve the traditional industrial structure, of sabotaging Soviet planning experience, of giving preference to thin rather than thick metal sheeting, of boosting production of small and light electric motors and machine tools, of opposing "the allegedly uneconomic exploitation of poor ores," and of holding up construction of ore-enriching plants. There was also talk of their having approved investments in the textile industry to a level eighteen times above those in ore mining, while the level of investment in the leather-working and rubber industries was supposed to have been twenty-one times higher. All ideas about a type of economic management that would have harmonized the interests of the state with those of enterprises were simultaneously nipped in the bud.

Today one cannot condemn out of hand the people who, in those exceptional times, succumbed to the oversimplified view of a socialist economy. After all, the Soviet socialization model was exempt from criticism by the very fact that it was linked with the name of Stalin. Indeed, his prestige being what it was, there could be no shadow of a doubt about the correctness of the model. Not just the men at the top, but also less prominent officials, economists, philosophers, men in industry — in fact, all of us — were subject to this spell. Naturally, this attitude was also rooted in the bureaucratic machine which, with its growing power, was bound up with the model. The turning point did not come until 1956, when the Soviet Communist Party held its 20th Congress. This was also the year that witnessed the first notable signs of growing economic difficulties in Czechoslovakia. At this point the economists began to realize that the economy was faltering and that while inputs were going up, performance was declining. When even then the men at the top still failed to grasp the situation, or tried to shut their eyes to it, the original errors began to depart more and more from the realm of common sense.

The years 1957 and 1958 saw the first outlines of what, six or seven years later, came to be called "the improved system of management." Incidentally, the very term "improved" reveals quite a bit about the abnormal conditions obtaining not so long ago. In fact, it was quite clear in the Czechoslovakia of the sixties that nothing short of a radical change in the system of management could possibly help. Nonetheless, the term "improved management" was forced on the economists. The idea, of course, was to persuade the public that the old methods had really been alright and that the outdated mechanism simply needed some improvement.

In a study prepared in 1958, I suggested that the roots of the country's economic ills lay in the underlying principles dictating that socialist commodity-money relations be artificially suppressed. It was evident that not even socialism could manage without a mechanism of prices, and of supply and demand. Yet for a full ten years the men at the top were incapable of bringing themselves to draw the necessary clear-cut conclusions from the increasingly precise findings of economic theory. The years 1959-1962 saw the application of a so-called planning methodology that sought to rehabilitate the law of value in some respects at least; nevertheless, the basic pattern still adhered to directive forms of management. What is more, a completed project for reform was already at the highest center of leadership when a newly published economics textbook, officially approved, came out with the biased and oversimplified contention that heavy industry offered the main source of technological advance.

In those days elder politicians were accustomed to appending the term "Leninist" to every decision, even the most senseless. Consequently one cannot let the opportunity pass to quote at this point a brief passage from Lenin's writings: "It is not the one who makes no mistakes that is intelligent. There are no such men, nor can there be. It is the person whose errors are not very grave and who is able to rectify them easily and quickly that is intelligent...a minor error can always assume monstrous proportions if it is persisted in, if profound justifications are sought for it, and if it is carried to its logical conclusion." (3)

The old guard in the political leadership, lacking theoretical grounding and unable to make their own analyses, were perhaps incapable of recognizing the grave errors. But when competent people had made the analysis, the rulers could at least have accepted the conclusions and adopted the appropriate decisions. Yet even that they failed to do. They clung to the old mistakes to the bitter end. And therefore the greater part of the economic losses, and of the moral and political losses too, can deservedly be laid at their door.

And now the time has come for us to consider the principle of the extensive economic model.

Enough has been said by way of introduction to suggest that development based on industrial expansion and mobilizing fresh manpower carries with it the built-in risk of stagnation. True, at first glance it appears to be an easy way; all that is needed is to siphon off from existing concerns all profits, all funds for accumulation (i.e., depreciation allowances), and even a substantial part of amortization funds, and to throw the resources so obtained into building new industrial capacities. But there is a snag: to build new factories from resources gained in this way we have to deprive ourselves of the means for modernizing existing plant. That is why a large part of our working class finds itself operating in an increasingly bad environment, using obsolescent techniques. Moreover, the Czechoslovak experience has shown that even the newly constructed plants fall short of the highest technological standards. The fact is that our new machines have been built to the same, or slightly improved, specifications as the old. To make matters worse, the new machinery has had to be manned largely by untrained labor, drawn primarily from agriculture, or from among housewives. Consequently, there has not been any marked advance in actual labor

productivity. Indeed, in some cases the performances of new
establishments have been poorer than those of the old factories
with outdated equipment because, with their skill and good organization, the workers in the latter have been able to hold their
own against the modest technological advantage of the new-
comers.

There is statistical evidence to support the above view: while
in 1957 industrial machinery and equipment older than ten years
amounted in value to 15 billion Czechoslovak crowns, six years
later, in 1963, the sum had nearly doubled (28 billion). (4) By
the beginning of 1968, the degree of obsolescence of capital assets had reached over 50 percent in the most neglected branches
of consumer industry. Capital assets in the textile industry are
obsolescent to the extent of 64 percent, in foodstuffs the figure
is 58 percent, in the leather-working and footwear industries it
is 54 percent, while in the printing trades technological obsolescence amounts to 59 percent. (5) There are real museum
pieces to be found in the consumer industries, dating from 60
to 80 years back. No wonder, then, that Italian and Austrian
workers achieve an average output per-man-hour that is one-
quarter to one-half higher than the Czechoslovak workers can
show. The West Germans and the British register performances
that are nearly double, and the Swedes, Swiss, Belgians, French
and Dutch surpass the Czechoslovak level by two-and-a-half
times. American operatives work at over four times the productivity rate of their Czechoslovak counterparts. (6)

To this discouraging picture we have to add the fact that in
investing the means at her disposal, Czechoslovakia has failed
to promote the most modern sectors where, on the other hand,
Western capital found the spearhead for future economic progress. That is to say, investment has not gone to sectors that
are typical for the scientific and technological revolution and
for the modern age, for instance, chemicals, electronics, instrument technology; the gainers have been the classical industrial branches of mining, heavy engineering, and metallurgy.
Of course, no industrially advanced country can dispense with
such undertakings, but the Czechoslovak speciality has been a

strong overdevelopment in these fields. The result has been
that socialism, which is considered as an advance on the scale
of social development, has been operating all the time on a production base belonging to the past century. The Czechoslovak
socialist system has been resting on a pillar of heavy industry
long since brought into being by private capital; capitalism,
however, had already discarded this relic of the past. No wonder that, under these circumstances, socialism has continually
come into conflict with an economic base that played its major
role in decades now long past.

The imbalance can also be illustrated by figures: in 1966
nearly one-fifth (19.5 percent) of the total volume of capital assets in Czechoslovakia belonged to engineering, while metallurgy accounted for 18 percent. Mining and fuel processing held
15.5 percent of the capital assets. (7) In contrast, the industries that have been traditional in this country fell far below
the latter level. Foodstuffs reached a bare half of the figure
for fuels (8.2 percent), and even the light consumer industries
failed to compete in this respect (13.1 percent of total capital
assets). Finally, the chemical and rubber-asbestos industries
constituted one of the weakest links (7.4 percent). (8) Nor was
the structure in this branch ideal. The most sought-after products of sophisticated industrial chemistry were relegated to
second place by the concentration on crude raw material production. To cite the figures: five years ago Great Britain had
already doubled the Czechoslovak output of plastics per capita,
and the level in West Germany was four times greater. And
while about one-third of the man-made fibers produced in the
United Kingdom, France and West Germany were already synthetic, the corresponding figure for Czechoslovakia was roughly
one-fifteenth (6.4 percent). (9) This fact alone indicates the uncompetitive nature of the country's textile goods.

This unfortunate state of affairs was largely the result of
arbitrary, unscientific, ill-considered decision-making, plus
primitive methods of planning. And the shortcomings of the
economy were magnified by unskilled management. But if we
go further into the workings of extensive development, we find

one Gordian knot after another appearing with iron logic. Extensive growth breeds pressures for fresh investment on a
grand scale, thereby putting a great strain on net capital for-
mation. This means that new construction projects swallow up
an inordinately large share of the disposable national income
at the expense of the portion available for consumption. And
since the new construction projects are not designed to serve
consumption, but to turn out steel, coal and heavy construction
units, the model cannot, with the best of intentions, conform to
the much-cited law about the all-round satisfaction of human
wants. On the contrary, the outcome is a sterile cycle of human labor and materials, senseless production for its own sake,
yielding no end effect. This strange paradox of an industrially
advanced country is to be seen most clearly in the field of heavy
industry. Heavy machine-building needs increasing supplies of
steel, forcing the steel works to expand production. But the
growing demand for metallurgical plant calls, in turn, for advances in heavy machine-building, which again requires more
steel, and so on without end. I remember writing once that the
sight of this merry-go-round can make an economist more diz-
zy than any reflections on the infinity of the Universe.

Inevitably all this adds up to rising claims on investment.
According to our calculations, in 1956-1960 an increment in national income of one Czechoslovak crown required investment
to the tune of 2.50 crowns. By 1961-1965 the corresponding figure was 9.50 crowns. (10) This alone indicates how ineffective
our investments have been, especially in recent years. What can
be more eloquent than the fact that within a single decade we
have had to raise investment expenditures fourfold to obtain the
same increment in national income? By the early sixties there
could be no doubt whatsoever about this fact: although we in-
vested 200 billion crowns in the national economy in 1961-1965
and increased the labor force by 300,000, the national income
was more or less stagnant. (11)

There is yet another disadvantage of extensive growth. Over-
financing of capital assets, channeled moreover primarily to
heavy industry, must sooner or later produce disproportions in

the consumer market, if for no other reason than that the pace of engineering and metallurgical plant construction cannot meet the needs of consumer production. In addition, the goods produced are less and less able to compete on the world market, leading inevitably to a shortage of foreign currency reserves. Ultimately the imbalance in the economy hits the capital goods market — raw materials, components, machinery and spare parts grow scarce, or at least are not to be had at the places and times required. And this situation is reflected in the average length of our construction operations. The old system of directive management forced building enterprises to take on more work than they could handle, regardless of the shortage of building capacities and despite the inadequate and, worst of all, the outdated equipment of the industry. Since these firms were fairly well equipped for earth shifting and the rough construction work, but lacked adequate facilities for the craft and finishing jobs, they naturally put most of their energy into the first stages of building. In any case, the old system operated in such a way that first-stage construction was highly profitable for the builders, while they had to expect losses on the finishing work.

As we shall see below, the inexpert management methods were incapable of offering people incentives in any branch of enterprise. We have looked at the picture in the construction industry, and we must bear in mind that every year spent on construction, especially in the case of industrial projects, heightens the danger that the new plant will be obsolete before it has been completed. For instance, a survey made in Czechoslovakia in the mid-sixties showed that while the standard construction period for power equipment is set at 37 months, the time schedule laid down by the very easygoing demands of the plan may be up to 65 months; the actual time, however, has averaged 71 months. The standard for fuel extraction works is 72 months, the plan allows for 107 months, and the reality is 122 months. (12) It is therefore no surprise to find that the average construction period for industrial plant in Czechoslovakia is five years, that is, twice as long as would be technically

possible in our country (13) and double or triple the time recorded by advanced capitalist countries.

Naturally, this unhappy state of affairs also exists in housing
construction. The shortcomings already mentioned, plus the
dispersion of construction workers over a wide range of sites,
have resulted in an eleven-month time schedule for putting up
one block of apartments in Prague. Before the war a block with
comparable interior facilities took five to six months to erect.
If we would rather not look to the West, we may note that the
Soviet Union achieves a housing construction rate that is twice
that of Czechoslovakia. (14)

All in all, this means that enormous resources of materials
and human labor have been frozen. At the end of 1966 there
were 17,908 projects under construction, and 109.6 billion
Czechoslovak crowns had been sunk in them. The balance of
the budgeted funds amounts to 101 billion, which at the above
rate of construction would mean work for a good six years. (15)
What is more, the chronic raw material shortage has led the
builders to accumulate vast stocks on the sites. For instance,
Ministry of Construction enterprises currently hold stocks sufficient for 116 working days, including supplies for some of the
finishing jobs that would keep them busy for 180 days. (16)

Confronted with such facts, one is impelled to ask what has
been the use of planning over the past twenty years in Czechoslovakia? How is it that a society that possesses all the pre-
conditions for truly scientific management shows this record
of slower, more costly, and inferior construction compared
with other industrially advanced countries? Everyone in Czechoslovakia knows what it means in practice — we have seen it
when traveling over our decrepit, neglected road and rail network, when submitting to treatment in inadequately equipped
hospitals, when standing in unending lines at the shops, when
observing the conditions under which our scientists work, or
when reading the recently published official news report that,
in number of dwellings per thousand of population, only Portugal and Yugoslavia are below us on the European ladder, although some statistics also put Spain lower.

There can therefore be no doubt whatsoever that Czechoslovakia will have to shift its emphasis in a relatively short period
from long-term investment in heavy industry to the sectors
that have suffered years of neglect. Some moves in this direction can already be noted. And all the building capacities that
we add will have to be concentrated in the sectors that are vital for our life today — in housing and in the broad range of
services that can save our time.

As this chapter ends, one is struck by the thought that it may
be better to cut one's coat to match one's cloth. Would it not
be more useful to have fewer, but more progressive and well-
equipped plants rather than a vast number of enterprises which
cannot measure up to sophisticated world standards? The final
answer to this question will have to wait for the second and,
especially, the third chapters of this book.

CHAPTER 2

HOW WE PRODUCE

A notable feature of previous reports on the state of the
Czechoslovak economy has been their remarkable oversimpli-
fication. The facts selected from the vast mass of available
data were those that would present the economy in the best possible light. Frequent mention was made, for instance, of the
country's occupying a leading place in the world in terms of industrial output, the rating being usually given as sixth or eighth.
Comparative tables showed that we held fourth place in Europe
for steel and pig iron production, sixth for cement, fifth for
hard coal mining, and second for brown coal. (1) There was no
question of doctoring the figures — they accurately represented
Czechoslovakia's position in the world. And yet appearances are
unfortunately apt to be deceptive. By simply pinpointing some
favorable figures we by no means give a true picture of the national economy. The yardstick of progress is not to be found in
the value of steel output per ton, or of the per-capita coal output, but first and foremost in the technological level at which
we develop our production potential. The ability to adapt to
structural changes in the world is a more reliable criterion
for deciding a country's place on the ladder of world economies
than, for example, figures for cement output. We have seen in
the first chapter that Czechoslovakia based her economy for
many years on traditions dating from the 19th century. We
started to hear timid references to the scientific and technological revolution in our country at a time when the industrially

advanced countries had long been swimming in the current of
these changes in civilization. The guardians of our ideological
purity labeled cybernetics as a bourgeois pseudoscience at a
time when the Western world was busy installing hundreds of
computers. Czechoslovakia has taken only the first steps in
automation, while the production of plastics, synthetic fibers,
and fertilizers is still in its infancy. If we want to discover
our real position in the world we shall have to start with these
none-too-encouraging facts. We shall then find, with some dis-
appointment, that our northern neighbor, the German Democratic Republic, has done much more to advance toward the
scientific and technological revolution and to make the essential structural changes in industry than we Czechoslovaks have
managed to do.

One thing, however, is beyond dispute — a tremendous production potential has been built up in Czechoslovakia, and this
in itself gives the country a top place in world statistics. We
can claim nearly 1.5 percent of world output (1.4 percent), and
per-capita output is more than 3 times the world average (3.2
times). (2) And so, although at the moment we are far from
satisfied with our industrial structure, although we would rather give priority to chemicals over the enormous blast furnace
capacities, we could in fact produce incomparably more than
we do from the wealth at our disposal. We are like beggars
living in the midst of great riches. Or, alternatively, we are
like rich men who are incapable of using the wealth they have
accumulated. In our own defense we should add, however, that
the old methods of management and planning gave Czechoslovak
producers very little opportunity to exploit the existing potential to its utmost. The administrative system of planned management that evolved in the Soviet Union in the late twenties
and early thirties proved, quite simply, to be unsuited to our
conditions — to a different environment and a different time.

Under that system, the main yardstick employed by the directive plan was a quite primitive index — that of gross output or,
in other words, the volume of output expressed in terms of
wholesale prices. By converting this gross output figure to

output per worker, the measure of performance, or index of labor productivity, was obtained. The prices used in these calculations were not formed on the market, but by bureaucratic methods at the center, and consequently there was always the chance that a highly effective product might be underestimated while some other product with low competitive qualities might appear to the enterprises as highly profitable. Since wage increases, bonuses, and recognition of merit in general were tied to such simplified criteria, we can hardly be surprised that enterprises, in their pursuit of gross output, were quick to concentrate on the products that would make things easy for them. Once we understand this mechanism, we can follow the whole pointless operation of the old management system as it departed more and more from considerations of common sense.

For instance, in their preoccupation with quantity measured in liters, tons and meters, enterprises lost sight of quality. In any case, the gross output index, backed up by dozens of auxiliary indexes, took no account of anything other than quantity. It was incapable of recording whether the economy was actually meeting consumer demand. Moreover, the market — the instrument that can register economic tremors with the accuracy of a seismograph, weigh supply and demand, and separate the rubbish from the top-quality goods — was kept inoperative. That is to say, the essential mechanism for letting the consumer's voice be heard had disappeared. In short, the economy had lost the feedback, as the cyberneticians would say, that in a healthy system can force producers to change their programs if their performance is consistently poor. With this lacking, all the links in the economic chain were on more or less the same footing, no matter whether sales were good or bad, whether operations were profitable or showing a loss. Enterprises could be sure of obtaining state funds for buying raw materials, paying wages, financing investments, regardless of whether their goods were piling up in the warehouses or reaping successes on world markets. Indeed, prosperous concerns were often in a more precarious position than factories that had only unsalable goods to show, because the successful firm is bound to keep its production program in line with demand at home and abroad, and program changes mean cuts in the volume of gross output. That is to say, output drops at least for a time while employees are acquiring the skills required by a new program.

At this point, then, we can understand at last why it was so difficult to find producers in Czechoslovakia who were ready to apply new discoveries — often really revolutionary inventions. As a typical example we may cite the jet loom, a machine that revolutionized textile technology by substituting a drop of water or a current of air for the shuttle. It was years before Czechoslovakia entered the world market with this striking technological innovation.

Now we can also understand why the purchasing power of Czechoslovak goods on the world market has been shrinking, why factories with excellent prospects for gaining a foothold in world trade went on working unconscionably long with obsolete design specifications. Data referring to the early sixties indicate that about one-third of design specifications (30.9 percent) were less than three years old; one-quarter dated from three to five years back (24.7 percent), and nearly another quarter had passed the acceptable age limit of five to ten years (22.8 percent). And this says nothing of the fact that a tenth of designs (10.1 percent) had originated ten to fifteen years earlier and over a tenth (11.5 percent) had passed the fifteen-year mark. (3)

When we did a check in the mid-sixties of fifty machine-building branches manufacturing four thousand product lines, the conclusions were no more encouraging; only some 39 percent of products came up to or topped world standards. The remaining two-thirds needed redesigning because they fell short of world standards (36 percent) or had to be scrapped because they were technologically outdated (25 percent). (4) The same picture emerged from a table showing the percentage reaching the world level at that time. While we could find some satisfaction in learning that 95 percent of vacuum tubes were up to standard, and some 40 to 60 percent of electrical instruments, machinery and equipment for the food industry, classical

components for the electronics industry, and plant for the textile and the sanitary goods industries could compare in quality
with similar products elsewhere, we could hardly be content
with the situation with respect to semiconductors, where statistics for the mid-sixties showed only 8 percent up to standard. Hydraulic elements (in the same comparison) could meet
world competition in a mere 21 percent of cases — and these
were products used in dozens of other branches of engineering,
where they served to depress the technological level again. (5)

Yet it would be unfair to blame the factories for this regrettable state of affairs. After all, an economy always has the enterprises and the final products that it creates by its own management methods. Consequently, if any direct responsibility
can be assigned for the pathologically low effectiveness of the
Czechoslovak economy, then it lies in the first place with the
old system of management. That system certainly failed to
create an atmosphere encouraging rapid technological development, although, in fact, Czechoslovakia has all the conditions
for such development. Moreover, since incentives had been
almost completely suppressed, one cannot wonder that the number of inventions registered fell far short of the figures for
many advanced countries in Europe. For example, data for
1964 record 56 patents per 100,000 inhabitants for Czechoslovakia, while in Britain the number was almost double (98), in
West Germany it was more than double (115), and in Holland it
was 127. In Sweden the comparable index for patents was four
times that of Czechoslovakia (204), and in Switzerland more
than five times (283). (6)

Another factor in creating Czechoslovakia's lag in relation
to the world's best was that the engineering industry, for instance, suffered from the mistaken belief that it had the status
of a great power. According to some figures it manufactured
close to three-quarters of the world assortment of engineering
products, operating in this respect at the level of a world power, but lacking, of course, the strong financial and research
capacity available in the big countries. It was, to say the least,
abnormal when statistics for the mid-fifties showed only a tenth

of a university student and a thousandth of a research worker per research project in engineering. We were trying to behave as if we were the United States, but in order to reach American standards in staffing all our projects we would have had, according to an article in the economic journal Hospodářské noviny, to put over half a million people into engineering research alone (7), assuming, of course, that we wanted to keep up with world standards over our entire range of production.

In the end, as things look today, we have gone beyond the limits of our capacity in dispersing our effort. Instead of concentrating on a few selected branches where we could really make headway on the world market, we have been manufacturing almost everything. In many branches our results have been meager, while we have tied up resources that could have been used to buy really first-rate know-how from leading foreign firms when our own efforts were inadequate. Ultimately we reached the paradoxical situation in which a great power in engineering like Czechoslovakia was suffering from a chronic shortage of machinery and equipment for vital sectors such as materials handling. While in 1965, 80 percent of handling work in the U.S. and West Germany was mechanized, the figure for Czechoslovakia was 20 to 22 percent; that is, four workers were needed where, with modern techniques, one could have done the job, and a total of 1,400,000 men and women had to be employed in such work. Moreover, while in the mid-sixties 8 percent of engineering output in the Soviet Union and France consisted of modern handling equipment, in Italy — 7 percent, and in the USA — 14 percent, the Czechoslovak figure was a mere 2.5 percent. (8)

There was still another unfortunate consequence of the utterly unsuitable management methods. The gross output index, which, as the yardstick for labor productivity, governed wage and bonus levels, led not only to technological stagnation but also to a shocking waste of materials, because the greater the bulk of raw materials a factory could manage to process, the greater the gross output it recorded. The inevitable outcome was a wanton waste of material and human labor. By way of

Diagram 1

comparison, whereas the wealthiest power of the capitalist
world, the USA, consumed 2,655 kg. of primary energy sources
to achieve $1,000 of gross domestic product, Czechoslovakia,
with no raw materials worth speaking of apart from coal, ura-
nium, timber, china clay and silica, consumed twice as much
(5,056 kg.). And while the United States, which had all the necessary raw materials at its disposal, used 186 kg. of steel per
$1,000 of GDP, the figure for small and by no means rich
Czechoslovakia was 435 kg. (9) Other countries, such as West
Germany, Italy and Japan, registered considerably lower

consumption of primary energy sources than the USA, while
not only American, but also Canadian, West German, British,
French and Italian works were more economical in their use
of steel than those of Czechoslovakia. Japan and West Germany
achieved 60 percent of Czechoslovak steel consumption, Sweden and the USA — 50 percent, Italy, the Netherlands and France —
40 percent, and Switzerland a mere third for the same end result. (10) What is more, consumption in all these countries
showed a long-term, lasting downward trend, while in Czechoslovakia the old system drove consumption along a steadily rising curve.

The complete unsuitability, indeed incompetence, of management under the old system is demonstrated more clearly by
these figures than by any lengthy dissertation. Unquestionably,
labor productivity measured by gross output (and therefore by
the amount of raw material processed) is incapable of revealing all the negative aspects of an economy. In the first place,
it ignores the labor inputs embodied in raw materials and power. Yet every ton of steel or iron saved obviously means a saving of labor in other sectors — in the foundries and the mines.
How paradoxical, indeed almost incredible, that in 1967 the bureaucrats proceeded once more to tie wage growth to this type
of labor productivity, and consequently to this shocking wastage. And this was done despite the fact that we had wanted, in
making the changeover to the new management system, to put
an end to just this senseless method of work. Not until 1968
was the way opened for the radical changes that have to start
first of all from this point.

Finally, all the economic problems created by extensive
growth — excessive manpower mobilization, unsuitable industrial structure with its accompanying lag in chemicals, sub-
standard machinery and an overall unsatisfactory technological
level — are projected into agriculture, the sector to which we
look as the key stabilizing factor for the entire economy.

Agriculture bore the brunt of the overrecruitment of manpower that is typical for extensive development. Between 1951
and 1964 alone, three-quarters of a million workers left the

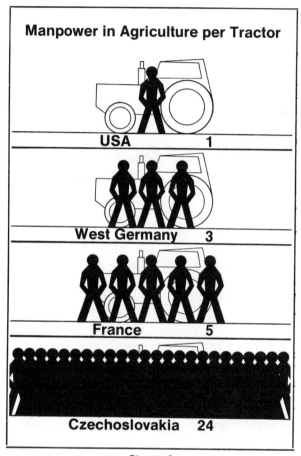

Diagram 2

land. (11) This drain would not be abnormal in itself, nor could we regard it as a negative factor, if it had been balanced by an influx of labor into industries working expressly for agriculture, for example, into the production of agricultural machinery and chemicals. This, at any rate, is how advanced countries compensate for a shrinking labor force on the land. In Czechoslovakia, on the contrary, there was an absolute drop both in farm labor and in the labor force of the entire agricultural-industrial complex. To make matters worse, the exodus was mainly among young people, precipitating a sharp deterioration in the age structure of farming compared with all other industries. To illustrate, about two-thirds of the labor force in manufacturing, mining, and construction falls into the 15- to 39-year-old group, while only a third of farm labor is in this age group. People over retirement age, that is, over 60, represent only 3 to 4 percent of manpower in the first sector, while in agriculture they make up over one-fifth (20.4 percent). (12)

Moreover, one must not think that mechanical equipment and supplies of chemicals were adequate to compensate farming for this handicap. In 1964 and 1965, for example, according to official statistics (13) the amount of pure nutrient per hectare of arable land was 147.2 kg. in Czechoslovakia, that is, about the same as in France (146.2 kg.) and rather less than in Denmark (173.4 kg.), while Austria was ahead of us by one-third (194.3 kg.), as was the UK (199.9 kg.). Switzerland put in twice the amount of nutrient (290 kg.), Japan (304.3 kg.) and West Germany (327.9 kg.) more than double, with Belgium (500.5 kg.) and Holland (556.8 kg.) registering three times the Czechoslovak figure.

Nor is the level of mechanical equipment all that could be desired. Taking the figures for tractors (1961-1965), for example,

	Most efficient machinery in Czechoslovakia at present	Level of foremost farms elsewhere
Tractor	55 hp.	60 hp.
	Productivity per shift	
Plowing	3-4 ha	8-10 ha
Grain combine harvester	16-20 ha	20-30 ha
Sugar-beet harvester	2.5 ha	5-6 ha
Potato lifter	2 ha	3-4 ha

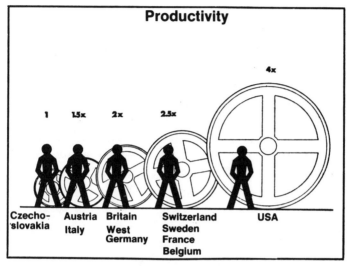

Diagram 3

	Czechoslovak average	Best current performance in Czechoslovakia	Foremost farms elsewhere
Grain harvesting	35–40	25	12–15
Fodder harvesting on arable land by cutter	16–20	12–15	5–8
Cultivation and harvesting:			
sugar-beet	350–450	ca 250	100–150
potatoes	250–350	ca 200	80–100
maize	100–160	ca 80	ca 26

we find that in Czechoslovakia the number of workers per tractor was 24, in France — 5, in West Germany — 3, while in the
USA there was exactly one farm worker per tractor. (14) (Of
course, these figures give no idea of the intensity with which the
tractors are utilized in collective farming.) Unfortunately, the capacity of our farm machinery also compares unfavorably with that
in other countries, as we can see from the table on page 64. (15)

The productivity of human labor in this area of work then
follows quite naturally. (16) The figures in the table on page 65
represent hours of work per hectare.

The columns of figures cited in this chapter demonstrate that
the principles of management so stubbornly adhered to by the
old guard among our politicians have failed to produce either
an economic structure that meets the needs of the day or a
growth rate of labor productivity that can reduce the lead held
by the Western world. Indeed, there has been a general failure
to ensure smooth operation of the economy. Neither in quantity
nor in quality has final output corresponded to the structure of
domestic and foreign demand. Consequently, on the one hand,
cash savings have been piling up, with consumers unable to
find the goods they want on the Czechoslovak market, and, on
the other hand, stocks of literally unsalable goods have been
accumulating in the warehouses. This symptom of economic
imbalance, the gap between supply and demand, is at bottom a
natural accompaniment to the path taken by the economy, a path
along which it could eventually do no more than stumble.

Current analyses have revealed, among other things, that of
the 45.2 billion Czechoslovak crowns deposited in private savings accounts at the end of 1967, a full 10 to 12 billion represented unsatisfied purchasing power. (17) The reverse side of
the coin is that we have stocks to the tune of some 200 billion. (18) Although raw materials and semifinished goods account for a part, a considerable share of this impossibly large
sum represents finished products. For instance, of the 10-
billion-crown increment in these stocks recorded in 1967,
80 percent were finished products. (19)

The only way out of this unhappy situation is to achieve a

complete renaissance of the market, the instrument best fitted to gauge the success or failure of enterprises. Equally vital is scope for independent enterprise — after twenty years of taking orders, management teams will have to accustom themselves to the hitherto unknown feeling that, without orders, advice, or approval from the top, they will be obliged to make full use of their own ideas. Indeed, with the market returning every failure, every lag behind world standards, with the precision of a boomerang, they will be forced to do so.

CHAPTER 3

How We Conduct Our Trade

CHAPTER 3

How We Conduct Our Trade

As a country with a big industrial potential, but a limited domestic market and no raw materials to speak of, Czechoslovakia would be hard put to maintain her economic existence if she did not develop intensive trade contacts with all parts of the world. Without the backing of Soviet raw materials resources, and without the great hinterland of markets in the socialist world, it would be impossible to plan our future development. Equally essential, however, are relations with the advanced industrial countries of the capitalist world, which fill in those notable gaps in our economy that we would find it difficult to cover from our own resources or, indeed, from those of our Eastern partners. In any case, the range of products is so wide in the world today that no single country (especially a country as small as Czechoslovakia) can be expected to embrace it all. And the world is advancing so rapidly that sooner or later all industrial countries will have to adjust to the requirements of growing specialization and international division of labor.

That is the background to the special position held by foreign trade in our economic life. And it is hardly surprising to find that this is the field where our economic problems are mirrored most accurately and also where we have the most sensitive barometer of the difficulties we are facing. Both the extent to which we have been caught napping by the start of the scientific and technological revolution, and the inappropriate

structure of our industrial production, which is intimately
linked with that transformation in civilization, are clearly projected in the field of foreign trade. The poor finishing of our
goods and the small returns we gain for labor expended are
felt only too strongly in our contacts with the rest of the world.
If, for example, we export a ton of metal sheeting for an average of 627 Czechoslovak crowns, and we buy the same item
abroad for nearly double the price, that is, for 1,232 crowns,
this fact alone shows that the value we add in processing raw
materials — which, moreover, are imported — is catastrophic-
ally low. This is no isolated example; nor is the price gap so
very pronounced. In the import and export of metal tubes, for
instance, the relentless "scissors" open even wider: while we
sell a ton of this item for about 1,000 crowns, we pay almost
five times the value in Czechoslovak crowns (4,958) for a ton
of imported tubes. (1)

A classic case of abnormally low value added in raw material processing is provided by the export of Czechoslovak timber. There are only two countries in Europe that export this
type of goods in its most primitive, raw state, and they are the
Soviet Union, with its boundless expanse of forests, and Czechoslovakia. It should be noted that timber constitutes nearly
28 percent of our exports to Britain, and 18 percent of deliver-
ies to Common Market countries. The timber is exported almost entirely in the form of raw lumber and sawn wood. Denmark, on the other hand, which has an incomparably smaller
raw material base than Czechoslovakia, reaped a profit of 45
million dollars on furniture exports in 1965 alone. (2) Thus,
Czechoslovakia's share in meeting the growing shortage of
wood in Europe is obtained in the least effective manner.

There are other factors that contribute to the net results of
our foreign trade. For instance, over the past twenty years we
have neglected the detail of packaging, which not only protects
goods but also sells them. Taking the costs of packaging in
Czechoslovakia as 100, we find the figure for France to be about
a quarter higher (122), for West Germany a third (132), for Sweden nearly a half (146), and for Britain nearly three-quarters (171).

Even higher on the scale are Canada at precisely two-and-a-half times the Czechoslovak figure, Switzerland — nearly three times (270), and the USA — over seven times (721). (3)

What is more, Czechoslovakia has been unable to offer the necessary service facilities for many of her products, not to mention the fact that the technological level is frequently poor. Yet a slight drop in technological quality is capable of depressing prices by a much large amount. This point may be illustrated in the case of two products chosen deliberately from other countries: (4)

	Technological level	Price
Straightening machine Norton 3/20 HW	100%	100%
Straightening machine Kieserling WROWN	80%	63%
Horizontal drill — West Germany Flauerwetzel BFN 80	100%	100%
Horizontal drill — Italy Ceruti B 75	96%	52%

Taking all this into account, we can understand why, in the case of many engineering products, we get only 50, sometimes 40, or even 30 percent of the prices obtained for similar articles by foreign competitors. And it can be no surprise to learn that while foreign trade is, for most advanced countries, a source of increments in the national income, in Czechoslovakia it fails to play that role. Such is the unhappy outcome of the fifties, of the old type of management, of extensive growth and the exaggerated efforts to be self-sufficient. In the endeavor to gain maximum independence from foreign markets, Czechoslovakia, small as she was, tried to produce everything, or almost everything, required for her economic life. In the end she stifled her considerable potentialities, reaching the point to which extensive development inevitably leads — disequilibrium in foreign trade and a chronic shortage of foreign currency. In the sophisticated world of today, self-sufficiency is not the way out; what is needed is concentration on serial production of certain lines, or on top-quality goods, and a small country can never achieve this with the one and a half million product types that Czechoslovakia is turning out today. It is essentially a matter of concentrating on producing the goods that are in demand in the world and where one has the chance of attaining really first-rate quality. Given the low costs of mass serial production, the prices our goods could fetch on the world market would compensate for the gap between our production costs and those current in other countries. In the case of top-quality products we can make up the difference by earning higher prices than those for run-of-the-mill goods. This is the only way to ensure an extra margin of profit on foreign trade. The earnings can then be used to supply our economy with imported goods that are manufactured at a lower cost and better quality than we can manage at home. That is the elementary ABC of trade which our captains of industry have ignored for close to twenty years.

In view of all this, one can hardly be surprised that Czechoslovak goods have been less and less able to compete in the world, that losses have been getting heavier from year to year, and that we have been compelled to step up our exports of domestic products to pay for a given volume of imported goods. Such is the price we have to pay for poor quality. For this reason alone we are now engaging in some export transactions that offer us no profit whatsoever. In some cases the earnings are not even enough to cover wage costs in production. Sometimes we fail to cover the full cost of raw materials and, to make matters worse, they are often materials that have been imported and processed at a heavy cost.

To quote some figures: while in 1954 we earned one dollar for 14 Czechoslovak crowns' worth of domestically produced goods, in 1967 we had to give 31 crowns' worth for one dollar (to be precise, 30 crowns 87 hellers). (5) There are big fluctuations around this average. Ministry of Foreign Trade figures

for 1967 (6) show that to earn one U.S. dollar we had to export
85 crowns' worth of sugar (the price includes a special sub-
sidy), 53 to 55 crowns' worth of metalware, coke or pig iron,
36 to 37 crowns' worth of stockings, knitwear, furniture, wire
and coking coal, and 33 crowns' worth of leather footwear.
There were a great many items on the other side of the 31-
crown average; for instance, the dollar-earning value of hard-
wood timber, molasses, hops, motorcycles, plywood, and glass
costume jewelry was 27 to 28 crowns, of chocolate and hydraulic jet looms — 25 crowns. Finally, such articles as Diesel
units, milling machines, pneumatic jet looms, china clay, and
gear-cutting and gear-shaping machines had a dollar earning
ratio of 1:17.

To complete the picture it would be well to cite an international comparison, made in 1965, of engineering export capacities: (7)

	Czecho-slovakia	The Nether-lands	Sweden	Italy
Machinery exported per employee, in dollars	1,465	4,578	4,627	3,693
Average per-kilogram price, in dollars	1.08	2.49	2.09	1.83
Share of engineering exports in total exports	37%	46%	27%	48%

We see from the above figures that Czechoslovakia, although
aspiring to be an engineering great power, actually exports
less than her competitors and, moreover, earns much less for
her work. Her counterparts earn three-quarters more, and in some
cases double, the amount per kilogram of exported machinery.
Finally, a comparison of these values as a long-term trend
might be useful: (8)

Average Per-Kilogram Price of Engineering Exports on
Capitalist Markets Earned by Czechoslovakia and
West Germany, 1936-1966 (in U.S. dollars) (9)

	West Germany	Czechoslovakia
Before World War II (10)	1.61	1.11
After World War II (11)	1.44	1.87
1961	1.70	1.05
1963	1.79	1.11
1966	1.99	1.00

These figures show that Czechoslovak engineering output is, in terms of its dollar-earning power, only half as effective as West Germany's and has even fallen below the level recorded for prewar Czechoslovakia. The reader may well ask why such ineffective products are put on the world market. Obviously, along with the financial loss, there is the damage to our good name. But extensive development and the overstressed effort to be self-sufficient were bound to lead to this. The inevitable outcome was to devalue Czechoslovak goods and to strain the trade balance to such a degree that we are now hard put to de- cide what export item we can risk eliminating without endan- gering our ability to import foreign goods and to meet our short-term commitments in the West.

At bottom the key to our foreign trade lies in the abnormal- ity of our economic relations. Whereas in every normally op- erating economy the full burden of business risk is borne by firms exposed to the pressure of a demanding world market, Czechoslovakia has allowed her socialist enterprises to exist apart from world competition. We can gain an understanding of this reality both from the price mechanism and from the whole concept of the country's foreign trade to date. As we know, prices were fixed on a long-term basis by the central bureaucracy. A factory computed its costs, putting them as high as possible, and the appropriate ministry, or the State Planning Commission, had no alternative but to approve the

computed price. The foreign trade enterprises then purchased
the products at these quite arbitrary prices and sold them
abroad with greater or lesser success, the risk being borne by
the state. The producer enterprises were supremely uninter-
ested in this end effect — they were completely in the dark
about world prices, about profits or losses recorded in foreign
trade dealings. One should add, of course, that our high production costs were of no concern to the outside world, and that
no one was willing to pay for the scandalous waste of raw materials in which we indulged. On the contrary, our massive
machines, well above normal weights, more often than not de-
pressed our selling prices. But after all, nobody worried much
about the losses because at the top, too, trade was seen as an
obligatory accessory to production rather than as a source of
national wealth. The approach was that we simply needed to
export a volume of products to meet the cost of essential imports — that is, our yardstick was quantitative, not economic.

Furthermore, the price relations led to such paradoxes that,
for instance, enterprises were most intent on getting products
on their export lists that appeared highly profitable in terms of
domestic prices. And the only reason for this was that they had
managed to persuade the central authorities to fix extra high
prices. In cases where the authorities had proved less accommodating we had difficulty in getting the goods concerned on the
world market. Yet in the first case the goods might show a
loss on export, while in the second the items might be quite
profitable export lines.

In any event, with wholesale prices more or less frozen and
bearing no relation to world prices, Czechoslovak enterprises
were unaware of all these circumstances. In short, the economy lacked the direct linkage that in a healthy economy tells
the producer in good time how he should conduct his operations.
Incidentally, this explains why, for example, all socialist countries are intent on building up their own automobile industries.
Under the given conditions of directive management, even
short-series production of automobiles may appear to be highly
profitable — until, of course, it is faced with competition from

giant firms abroad.

In order to avoid such confrontations, the Czechoslovak economy lets many highly unprofitable products escape to the less
sophisticated markets, which in no way contributes to stability,
if only because such trade is usually conducted on credit and
the terms are steadily deteriorating. The backflow periods on
big capital investments are doubled or trebled in most cases.
Production payrolls have to be met, but it may take eight or
ten years before the outlays are covered by the corresponding
goods. This is the source of one of the inflationary channels.
And yet our claims on foreign debtors are not in excess of
what our economy should be able to carry. Indeed, countries
of our size in the West often take on more. The following comparison for 1965 will give the full picture. (12) While credit aid
to developing countries amounted to 2.38 dollars per capita in
Czechoslovakia, the average for the Western countries was
15.6 — ranging from 2.2 (Portugal) to 28.5 (USA). But for an
unbalanced economy even quite small credits can prove an
enormous burden, not to mention the fact that a less demanding
market fails to exert pressure toward profitable performance.
And that is the crucial problem today.

The only action that can help keep the balance of payments healthy and speed up the growth of our national income is to step up highly effective export trade to markets
where we can find, in return, goods for domestic consumption that we can import as quickly and on as favorable
terms as possible.

A radical solution must therefore be sought first of all in a
direct impact by foreign competition on our industry. This was
also the purpose of steps — initiated when the new management
system was officially introduced — to allow foreign prices to
impinge directly on our producer enterprises. But the protectionism of the past persists. Successful enterprises still find
part of their earnings cut by deductions, while the less successful are bolstered by allowances to enable them to venture, with
their existing cost levels and quality, to offer their goods on

foreign markets at all.* And so, to this day, world competition is not really making any appreciable impact on our enterprises. However, when the firms now enjoying protection have to bear the consequences of any losses they incur, they will at last be forced to look for effective production programs and for profitable export lines. On the other hand — and this is even more important — we shall steadily reduce the deductions from the earnings of the successful concerns. We shall have to let them keep a bigger share of their profits for use in expanding their production potential.

Only when uncompetitive enterprises realize that a date has been set for the end of doping, will they lose the peace that they have enjoyed hitherto; then they will see on the horizon the moment when they will have to stand on their own feet. In the meantime, however, the consumer industry is reaping 2 billion crowns in subsidies, mining around one billion, and heavy industry some 900 million. (13)

Another essential step will be to clear out of the way the mainstay of protectionism — our ill-conceived foreign trade monopoly. Of course, none of us has any doubt about the need for the state to conduct its foreign currency policy and to use economic instruments to safeguard the balance of payments. Today this is accepted policy in capitalist countries, too, and a socialist government intent on planning development over the long run has all the more reason to apply it. But we must stop confusing the issues. We have to become accustomed to the idea that there are other ways of conducting foreign trade than

---

*In computing, at the official exchange rate, the prices actually obtained on the foreign market, some items show big profits while others show losses (price lower than production cost). By taxing the high profits, the state gets funds to subsidize the transactions requiring support. Had the reform abolished all subsidies at a stroke, many enterprises would have had to close down; however, the reformers aimed to do away with these "deductions" and "allowances" slowly but surely.

our monopoly system whereby trade operations are exclusively reserved for special corporations which, moreover, are staffed by people versed in all sorts of professions but not in commerce. Indeed, neither I nor any other Czechoslovak economist can assess today the extent to which our failures on world markets are due to the goods we offer and how much the people on the job bear a share of the blame. We know that they have often grasped at the easiest outlets, but when competition and incentives tied to results are lacking, we cannot expect miracles. What is needed is that producers themselves have an interest in effective exporting and importing; they must make their own way in the commercial sphere and shoulder the full risk of their sales operations. Only then will we see a radical improvement in this sector as well, to the benefit of industry and all of us.

CHAPTER 4

HOW WE LIVE

The first three chapters of our evaluation — and indictment — of the directive management system have shown the weak points in Czechoslovakia's investment record, production, and foreign trade. We have seen that development under the antediluvian methods of management was bound to run aground in terms of technological level, with a consequent loss in competitiveness. The methods that the old-time politicians clung to out of sheer incompetence also failed in the sphere of organization. Not surprisingly, when losses were running in the billions, a decline in working morale seemed to be a negligible factor. In any case, this factor can also be laid at the door of the political veterans who, to the very last, persisted in applying their outdated recipes, elaborated ad absurdum, although they had never been and never could be successful under Czechoslovak conditions.

All this naturally had its effect on living standards, since sooner or later the country has to foot the bill for any abnormal and inexpert management of affairs. And the bill we have incurred is quite large. The conservative elements in our country need to be reminded of this when they go around muttering threats about "not allowing anyone to lay hands on the achievements of the working class." This fourth part of our stocktaking should also ask these people to tell us whether they think that the level attained — so inadequate to twenty years of work — is one of the achievements of the working class. Our economists

really cannot be expected to go on making comparisons with
the level of thirty years ago. Economic growth is not, after all,
peculiar to Czechoslovakia — almost all countries in the world
have advanced during the three decades since 1938. The statistics of Chad, for example, undoubtedly record many encouraging figures. If we wish to draw comparisons it would be pref-
erable to look at the distance covered by other European countries against which we would like to measure ourselves. In
short, the yardstick for 1968 should not be the 1938 level; we
should see our progress in relation to that of the advanced
world.

The first point to be noted is that both nominal and real wages
have shown a substantially steeper upward movement in other
countries. During our first five-year plan — 1949-1953 — the
average annual wage increment still amounted to 6 percent. By
the time of the second five-year plan — 1956-1960 — the increment had dropped to 4 percent, and in the first half of the sixties, when flagging growth had reached stagnation point, the figure was just 2 percent. These rates may be compared with
those of our nearest neighbors, Austria and West Germany. In
1955, average earnings in the socialist sector (excluding cooperative farms) in Czechoslovakia were 1,186 crowns. By 1965
the figure had risen to 1,463 crowns, that is, the Czechoslovak
wage level had risen by about one-quarter. Over a comparable
period — 1954-1964 — workers' wages in Austria went up from
1,351 Austrian shillings to 2,840 shillings, that is, they more
than doubled. And in West Germany the average growth of
workers' wages was two-and-half times over the same ten
years, reaching 805 DM by 1964. (1) Naturally, prices in Austria and West Germany also rose, but we find that our neighbors kept their lead in real wages as well. Between 1954 and
1965, real wages went up by 37.5 percent in Czechoslovakia, by
54 percent in Austria, and by 93 percent in West Germany. (2)

But to make the picture as clear as possible we shall have to
convert the figures to a common denominator. We can do this
by comparing the GNPs of the countries concerned in dollars.
There is some difficulty at present in fixing an accurate exchange

rate for the Czechoslovak crown and the dollar. The black market rate, which of course bears no relation to the true rate, is 1:36, but even the official rate of 1:7 is unreal. In the following table we have taken the rate of 1:18 because a ratio between 1:17 and 1:19 seems nearest to the actual relation of the two currencies. And now we can proceed to compare the per-capita GNP for 1966 in dollars: (3)

Sweden	2,405
West Germany	1,740
France	1,734
Belgium	1,683
UK	1,652
Austria	1,191
Italy	1,043
Czechoslovakia	1,038

In Czechoslovakia, as we know, investments were swallowing up a growing share of the above sum, at the expense of personal consumption. In 1937, and in 1948, personal consumption accounted for over two-thirds of the GNP, but by 1966 (in terms of prewar prices of 1937) it was down to about a half. (4) Incidentally, this share is lower than in any advanced country of the capitalist world. The gap emerges from the following comparison of the percentage share of personal consumption in the GNPs of several European countries in 1966: (5)

Belgium	64.9
France	63.7
Italy	63.1
UK	61.8
Austria	59.8
West Germany	57.1
Sweden	56.3
Czechoslovakia	53.4

Since Czechoslovakia's GNP is perceptibly lower than that of many capitalist countries, and since the share going to personal consumption is substantially lower than elsewhere, our calculations will obviously yield results that throw an even less favorable light on our living standards.

The discrepancy is especially marked when we compare the time that a Czechoslovak worker has to expend in order to earn the means to buy a product type that his West German colleague, for example, can acquire in an incomparably shorter period. Although such time comparisons can never be quite accurate because goods offered in Czechoslovak and West German shops cannot be precisely equated, these rough data do provide an instructive illustration: (6)

	West German worker	Czechoslovak worker
	Working hours	
TV set	133	470
Sewing machine	88	287
Portable typewriter	32	129
Transistor radio	12	117
Pair of shoes	6	17
Pair of ladies stockings	0.8	5.8
17.5 kg. assorted meat	27.4	53.9
1 kg. chocolate	1.5	10.5
Can of crab meat	0.7	1.4
Can of Nescafé	0.5	4.2
Frankfurters (canned)	0.4	1.6
Can of strawberries	0.3	1.2

Nonetheless, Czechoslovakia's homes are not too badly equipped: in 1967, 67.6 percent of households had washing machines, 44.8 percent had refrigerators, 66.3 percent had TV sets, and 11.7 percent owned automobiles. (7) Czechoslovakia comes well up to world standards with respect to quite a number of items. For instance, the number of TV sets per capita exceeds the figure for several countries, although Britain, Belgium, France, and Austria are well ahead. We are behind in refrigerators, and especially in ownership of private automobiles. While the world average is 24 people to one car, in Czechoslovakia there are 35. For comparison we cite figures for some other countries: (8)

USA	2.4	UK	7.9
New Zealand	3.4	Switzerland	8.1
Canada	3.4	Belgium	8.6
Australia	3.5	West Germany	8.8
Sweden	5.2	Norway	9.3
France	5.9	Finland	13
Denmark	7		

Forecasts suggest that by 1975 Czechoslovakia should have one car per 15 people, by 1980 — 10, and the ultimate goal has been set at 1:6. (9)

On the whole we cannot complain about the calorific value of our food: while in West Germany the daily calorie consumption averaged 2,914 between 1961 and 1965, and in Austria 2,960, the figure for Czechoslovakia was 3,110. (10) But the main, and as yet unsolved, problem is the composition of our national diet, which is only gradually approaching the accepted standard for Western countries. For example, in 1963-1964 the Czechoslovak population consumed 170 kg. of flour per capita. The Austrian consumer averaged 102 kg., and the West German 75 kg. Consumption of meat in Czechoslovakia, amounting to 58 kg. per person, was exactly 5 kg. less than in Austria and 6 kg. less than in West Germany, and the per-capita egg consumption of 9.3 kg. was about one-third below the Austrian and West German levels, while consumers in the latter two countries eat twice as much cheese as the Czechoslovaks (2.3 kg.). (11)

True, meat consumption was up by 1967 to 63 kg. per person (12), approaching the level of Belgium and Austria. Nevertheless, our diet is still not adequate by health standards. It is

not clear whether the blame lies more with the country's traditional eating habits or with the high prices of food. Of course,
the prices at which one can buy a thousand calories vary. In the
mid-sixties, for example, a Czechoslovak consumer could get
his thousand calories in flour at a cost of 1.08 crowns, or in
sugar at 2.35 crowns, while if he wanted the same calories in
milk it would cost him 3.44 crowns, processed cheese — 8.07
crowns, and pork — 8.44 crowns. The same calorie value could
be obtained from 12.05 crowns' worth of eggs and 17.72 crowns'
worth of beef. (13) Naturally, the poorer families have to rely
on foodstuffs in the lower price ranges.

   At all events, a good slice of our personal consumption goes
for foodstuffs. Taking a comparison for 1964, we find that
Czechoslovakia tops the list in this respect among several advanced industrial countries of Western Europe: (14)

Percentage Share of Expenditures on Foodstuffs in Total Personal Consumption

Sweden	22.8
UK	33.4
France	36.6
West Germany	36.8
Austria	40.4
Italy	46.4
Czechoslovakia	50.0

   In addition to high prices, another factor in producing this
big share of foodstuffs in our family budgets seems to be the
shortage of other attractive goods and satisfactory services.
The result is that, on the average, people consume more food
than in other countries, although the prices are relatively
higher. We have much less left over for cars, electrical goods,
holidays abroad, and the other items that are usually included
in private expenditure under the heading "sundry expenditures."
We spend a smaller share on such things, although our average
spending on heating, lighting, and rent is below the average for

Western countries. Comparing the "sundry expenditures" in
family budgets for 1964 in percentage shares, we find: (15)

Sweden	39.5
UK	32.2
France	30.7
Italy	29.0
Austria	26.2
West Germany	25.5
Czechoslovakia	20.0

However, if the unfortunate state of the economy can be said
to have hit some sectors more than others, then it is the housing standards, the neglected communications network, the utterly inadequate range and quality of services, and the poorly
equipped educational and health services that show the effects
very clearly. True, we have some facilities that some citizens
of the West may envy — free medical care, numerous doctors
— but, on the other hand, we are astonished to learn from a
comparison of the health expenditures of twenty-three countries that Czechoslovakia was next to last on the ladder —
ahead of Tanganyika. And while the number of health personnel
per 100 hospital beds is 100 in the Soviet Union and 180 in the
USA, the figure for Czechoslovakia is 53. (16)
We are also wont to boast in our statistical surveys about
our cheap rents. But we can hardly be satisfied with the state
of our housing. The fact is that 43.4 percent of Czechoslovak
citizens live in overcrowded homes, which means, by the Czechoslovak standard, that in such dwellings there are less than
eight square meters per person. (17)
What is more, we have noted in the present decade that there
is only one country in Europe in which housing deteriorated between 1950 and 1961, and that country was Czechoslovakia. (18)
The number of dwellings per 1,000 of the population dropped
from 293 in 1950 to 280 in 1961. (19) Only in 1965 was there an
advance to 294.
And while in 1956 Czechoslovakia was thirteenth among

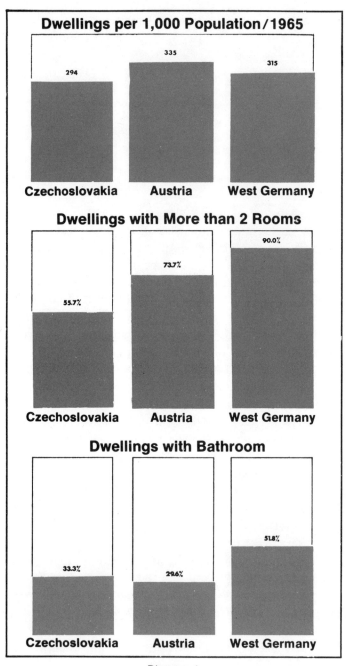

Diagram 4

twenty-three countries in the intensity of housing construction, she had sunk to eighteenth among twenty-five countries surveyed during the first five years of the 1960s. (20) In 1965 her position was down to twentieth. (21)

What has emerged here is, in fact, the logical outcome of what we have termed extensive development. As we have traveled along that road, the overinvestment in industry has even deprived us of space for living.

Current calculations indicate that if we are to catch up with the advanced countries of Western Europe in this field and achieve an annual increment of living space equal to theirs, we must build around 150,000 dwellings of our average size annually. (22) However, far from building this number in a year, the total for the past two years (1966 and 1967) was 153,373. (23) At this rate we would prolong the solution of our housing crisis well into the next century, and probably we would never solve it at all. We will return to this subject, adding only at this point that the housing question does not depend on good or bad planning figures; it is directly linked to the principles in accordance with which the entire economy is managed. That is to say, instead of enormous numbers of ineffective plants, it is imperative to build far fewer, but highly effective plants, thereby enabling us to concentrate all increments in construction capacities in housing.

However we may view the situation, our low housing standards and especially the lack of homes for young married couples have presented us with a figure that constitutes the strongest indictment of the pre-January system: there have been over 800,000 abortions during the past ten years. (24) Although there are other factors at work here, this figure is in itself something of an overall indicator of the regrettable economic situation. Czechoslovakia has actually sunk to one of the last places in population growth.

The compilers of demographic statistics portray population movements by means of the so-called tree of life, which should spread out gradually from the older to the younger age groups. During the present century, however, our tree has been hit by three major crises. The first was World War I, which made a dent in four annual age groups. Then came the Depression, taking its toll of six age groups, and the third downward plunge is with us today. In 1965 the statisticians calculated that if we were to start improving our population situation immediately, the inroad on the tree of life would already have affected nine age groups. (25) Yet, as we know, far from improving, the situation is still deteriorating.

Alongside the housing crisis, the high employment rate among women undoubtedly contributes to this unfortunate state of affairs. This, too, in its way is an indicator of the situation in Czechoslovakia today. That is, we have managed to maintain a fairly good standard of living thanks to the work of millions of women, whose contribution to family budgets amounts to 30 to 40 percent of all income. And when real wages are stagnant or falling there is always a tendency for more members of a family to go out to work. The point can be illustrated by comparing Czechoslovakia with two countries chosen at random: while in Czechoslovakia over one-half (58.6 percent) of married women were employed at the start of the decade, the figures for the United States and Sweden were roughly one-third (33.6 and 34 percent respectively). (26) Or consider this: between 1948 and 1964 the labor force in Czechoslovakia increased by 865,000, and 760,000 were women. Yet under the old management system the economic effect of this increment was highly questionable, not to mention the fact that in 1961 a full 83.8 percent of employed women had no more than elementary education. (27)

I have no wish to use these figures as an argument against the employment of women. But I do believe that the motive for women to enter into employment should be purely the desire for emancipation and not economic pressure. Under no circumstances should the rate of employment overstep the boundary beyond which the stability of population growth and the health of future generations is threatened. Moreover, in a country which, thanks to ill-considered navigation of the economic ship, is incapable of meeting the growing need for adequate services, overemployment of women can be a veritable catastrophe. The truth is that the stability of the nation's population is most gravely threatened when the communications network is allowed to decay, when women are forced to stand in lines for hours to buy the staple foods, and when the family has to carry the entire burden of the household itself. If a woman in Czechoslovakia has to waste one to two hours a day in getting to and from work, another two hours on household chores, and then loses a great deal of time because of the lack of services, one cannot be surprised that she is left with a minimum of time for bringing up her children.

A few facts will serve to illustrate the state of affairs in the "tertiary" sphere of services. Whereas in Czechoslovakia in 1967 about a third of the active population was employed in this sphere (33.2 percent), in Sweden the figure was already 41 percent of the total labor force in 1961. In Britain almost half the active population (49 percent) was in such employment by 1963, and in France — 40 percent by 1962. (28)

A clear-cut picture emerges from a series of data concerning all aspects of this, the weakest aspect of life in Czechoslovakia. Statistics relating to the mid-sixties, for instance, give the number of people commuting to work as 2,300,000. The average commutation by train is given as 25 kilometers, and by public road transport — 10 kilometers. (29) Although the distances may not seem great, the time wasted was inordinate, not to mention the discomforts involved. Taking just a few figures for municipal transport, for instance, we find that investment in the Prague area amounted to 23 Czechoslovak crowns per capita per year between 1954 and 1965, while in Stockholm the annual per-capita expenditure between 1952 and 1955 was 67.50 Swedish crowns, equivalent to 94.50 Czechoslovak crowns. And while in Prague a mere 8.50 crowns per capita per year were devoted to public transport, the corresponding figure for Stockholm was 56 Swedish crowns in 1963, equivalent to 78 Czechoslovak crowns. (30)

The lag in retail trade and municipal services may be illustrated by the following table: (31)

	Czechoslovakia	Western Europe
Employees per retail trade unit	2.5	3.2
Inhabitants per retail trade employee	95.4	28.3
Inhabitants per retail trade unit	237	93

A similar picture emerges from a comparison of the number of inhabitants per workshop in the trades and crafts: (32)

	Inhabitants per Workshop		
	Czecho-slovakia	German Democratic Republic	Federal Republic of Germany
Metalworking	4,028	525	430
Woodworking	6,626	869	768
Clothing	5,214	1,050	894
Leather-processing	7,553	1,176	1,413

Thus the country faced a most difficult situation in many branches of the economy, and the blame lay both with the old management system and with the men at the helm who held so stubbornly to the old course. One can hardly be surprised, in these circumstances, that they had to pick and choose the facts and figures to be published in order to present as optimistic a picture as possible. In those days the man in the street used to tell an anecdote about a breakdown in communication between the senses of hearing and sight — what he saw bore no resemblance to what he heard. Although there were comparative studies of the economic ills that were troubling people, such reports were not intended for public consumption. And at this point it would be appropriate to ask the politicians who relinquished their power on January 5, 1968, and are still proclaiming

themselves the guardians of working-class "achievements,"
whether they consider the results cited above as part of their
achievement too. Do they think that the present standard of
living, the housing shortage, the poorly equipped health services, the polluted rivers, and the rest represent gains for the
working class? It would also be relevant to ask the authors of
illegal leaflets, who are rather belatedly anxious about the "better future" for our children, whether they were thinking about
that future in the days not so long ago when, thanks to their efforts, the country was incapable of ensuring even the simplest
reproduction of its housing, its forests and land resources, and
of entire sectors of the consumer industries, when we were
living, one might say, at the expense of that "better future"
that had been promised.

This legacy will not be easy to cope with, and we shall have
to start with the management of our economic undertakings
rather than with the immediate ills. After all, efficient services do not come into being because sensible economists want
them but because, with the advance of the scientific and technological revolution, manpower is released to this sphere from
industry. Consequently, as long as economic growth depends on
swelling the volume of industrial construction and on mobilizing
new manpower, it is hard to envisage first-class services. The
first step may be — and indeed must be — to get the new economic system into full working order. There is good reason to
view this primarily as the lever that should turn the Czechoslovak economy into the stream of the scientific and technological
revolution. Its role in curing our present difficulties takes second place because that depends on the first, far more essential role.

The way forward involves major changes in the nature of our
civilization and a radical new departure in production. Here,
too, we shall find the road toward higher earnings. While exaggerated wage demands would not today yield a rise in living
standards, but would simply mean circulating worthless paper,
by switching the economy to another course we can gain the financial and industrial structure on which to base our future, the
quality of our life, and our standing in the world.

CHAPTER 5

HOW WE MANAGE OUR ECONOMIC LIFE

CHAPTER 5

How We Manage Our Economic Life

Technology, which may but need not be a menace to humanity, has been considered in hundreds of philosophical works.
There have also been innumerable debates on the subject. I
have no desire to enter into all that. It merely occurs to me
that man is menaced far less by technology than by unskilled
management that wields the technological potential in an ama-
teurish way. Indeed, the example of Czechoslovakia is warning
enough. An architect who designs a prefabricated house is
bound to respect the laws of statics. Yet the veterans of Czechoslovak politics did not hesitate to handle the economic orga-
nism, with all its complexity, while calmly ignoring all economic laws. When the arm of the law catches you driving without a license you are subject to strict penalties, but the men
who played fast and loose with Czechoslovakia's economic potential, and therefore with the fate of fourteen million people,
were not required to produce any proof of their qualifications
for the job. The result can be seen from the stocktaking presented in the four preceding chapters, and this is also the
source for the conclusions we are now drawing after the bitter
experience over the years. There is therefore no question that
the starting point for a revival of the Czechoslovak economy
has to be in the sphere of management.

Probably few people would doubt that January 5, 1968, opened
up unprecedented opportunities for Czechoslovakia, including
the prospect of making a thorough overhaul of our undertakings

99

with a vigor we have never known before. And this does not apply to the economic sphere alone.

I cannot refrain, in this connection, from a few reminiscences of days long gone when a similar opportunity to pursue a special Czechoslovak road to socialism was first under discussion. More than twenty years have passed and, as we know, that first great opportunity came to nothing. The fact is that — not through our fault alone — we allowed it to slip away bit by bit.

Leafing through the Statistical Yearbook will convince us that in the postwar years we made rapid advances both in output and in the living standard of the people. Moreover — possibly as the first nation to do so — we developed a highly democratic mode of planning. Hundreds of experts, the personnel of our enterprises, the true captains of our industry, took part in managing the economy, and alongside them were representatives of political parties and of bodies such as the trade unions, the Industrial Union, the Farmers' Union, etc. The results surpassed expectations: big nationalized enterprises were operating in Czechoslovakia, and they were still behaving as business undertakings; indeed, they were even able to compete with major concerns in the West. The country's Communist economists were looking for progressive methods of management suited to our conditions and requirements, and they were beginning to gain footholds in the undersupplied European market.

Nonetheless, there came a sudden and radical change. Little Czechoslovakia, lying in the heart of the European continent, was to bear all the cruel blows of the Cold War and to be confronted with the aberrations that the fifties — with all that period implied — placed in the path of a rather small and insignificant country. The first ventures in progressive management were abandoned. Czechoslovakia went over to an administrative, centralized type of planning and management that had evolved in a different environment, under different conditions. As we have seen in the foregoing chapters, we succeeded by degrees in killing enterprise initiative and, instead of healthy socialist business enterprise, the entire country became involved

in chasing high output targets. The plans simply encouraged
this abnormal type of operation. The firms increasingly lost
sight of their own needs, and those of others, submitting meekly
to the arbitrary directives, advice and orders from the top. The
authorities at the center literally confiscated all financial resources in the factories, allotting them as they saw fit to investment, raw materials, and wages. With their monopoly of
wisdom, they alone decided what should and should not be left
to the enterprises down below. And so in time the unhealthy
practices, which could at best be justified in time of war, became a set and indisputable routine. The people at the top stip-
ulated the size of the labor force, the level of gross output,
which branches should be given priority, and which should not.

The outcome was that the working people, who were supposed
by law to be the co-owners of socialist property, in fact lost
this sense of ownership. Big units that had once prospered even
on the world market were disbanded, and over their heads there
grew up a giant structure of departmental ministries and central administrations; the unending chopping and changing to
which this organizational structure was subjected had no impact on the men down.below on the job.

Most important of all, the producer's interest in the market
disappeared. It was bound to disappear when enterprise performance was completely divorced from the market. The enterprises had to go cap in hand to their superiors for everything they wanted, which in itself implied a total separation of
production from market results. Consumer wants were really
a matter of indifference — except to the consumers, of course.
And we were all consumers.

The enterprises were transformed into cogs in the economic
machine, to be manipulated by the men at the center and forced
to provide the highest output at the lowest costs — without regard, naturally, to the end effect. So they adopted the most obvious mode of defense: they understated their potentialities and
overstated their needs. They knew, after all, how the authorities went about things, automatically prescribing higher outputs
than enterprises were willing or able to manage, and blue-

pencilling their demands wherever possible. And there evolved a mechanism for deception on a grand scale, of not showing one's hand, and this was the only sphere in which people's initiative could really develop to the full. The consequence was that the Czechoslovak economy lost its last asset — objective information about needs, reserves, and potentialities.

What is more, all appointments of management personnel in industry were made from the top, along the same lines as the allotting of plan assignments down the ladder. No one bothered about the needs of individual units on the lower rungs, or about the conflicts in which they might be involved. There were not even any alternatives presented so that employees might make a choice. A central decision was above all a command. The actual results and possible impact were ignored. As regards the plan, all that had to be done was to state the percentage fulfillment of targets. As regards management personnel, the authorities were content if people showed "devotion" and were politically reliable.

It was, however, a rather curious notion of reliability. A director was expected to be loyal first of all to the holders of power, who in turn identified their power positions with the existence of socialism as a system of society. But, in any case, what had devotion to socialism in common with the nepotism and wire-pulling that were the chief factors in making these appointments?

Education and experience were quite minor considerations. Those with the power evidently forgot that the interests of the working people could best be defended by experts capable of tuning up the capacities entrusted to them to such high performance that a socialist enterprise, too, would make a superior showing. As we know, however, no one was interested in a detail like that.

But for Czechoslovakia today such an interest is imperative. Anyone lacking specialist training and adequate knowledge, experience, and ability cannot meet the political requirements either, if only because he would be incapable of managing a business concern to the benefit of the consumer and in the interests of the worker, whose earnings will depend more and more on whether a management team makes faulty or well-considered decisions.

Prior to January 5, 1968, wherever one looked it was really only power that mattered. The screen of selection was adjusted to let through the people who showed promise of supporting the men at the top. And any successful candidate who did not feel too sure of himself simply repeated the accepted practice — he chose his staff from among people he could rely on. As far as possible they were even less qualified, amateurs guaranteed not to outshine their chief.

In the long run the old power system molded people at all levels in its own image. It created conditions that permeated deeply into the consciousness of the nation.

That is how we were shaping our life and way of managing things when the West had already discovered new sources of growth in the scientific and technological revolution. In the West it was recognized, along with other things, that the days were long past when someone could take a director's seat just because he held a controlling block of shares in his safe. In the interests of self-preservation the owners of concerns voluntarily vacated the directors' offices to make way for managers, because they had been convinced in practice that the biggest property owners are not necessarily the best directors. And that is the rule rather than the exception. Yet Czechoslovakia was filling its top posts according to the yardstick of power. This was at a time when capitalist countries were setting up giant institutions for training management personnel. Capitalism had grasped a fact that our social order should have seen long before, namely, that management is a difficult and exacting profession calling for knowledge and experience plus some measure of talent as well. It calls for the ability to take risks, the art of handling people, the capacity for making decisions and choosing one's colleagues. That is why the major capitalist concerns now choose their young executives from among the best university graduates and with the aid of sophisticated psycho-technological tests. Those selected are put into special courses to learn about modern marketing methods, the sociological and psychological aspects of management, the use of computers, and the latest management know-how. People trained in this way are then sent to work for a time with foreign firms. They go through every department of their own concern and are finally assigned as assistants to executive personnel. The result is a pool of real managers, ready at any time to step into top posts.

One example out of many will suffice to illustrate the care devoted in the United States to selecting top personnel. The American Telephone and Telegraph Company has fifty centers for personnel selection, each of which costs around a quarter of a million dollars a year. This firm is undoubtedly motivated by the accepted principles of good business and is putting its capital into something that it knows will bear rich profits in the long run.

In the United States, 600,000 people go through management refresher courses each year. This represents a vast reserve of potential managers. Fifty thousand students pass through the AMA (American Management Association) courses at Hamilton, New York alone each year, and they range from departmental heads to the general directors of big firms. (1)

In Czechoslovakia, on the other hand, there is an unbelievably low skill structure among socialist management teams, with an absurdly weak level of management in the enterprises as the most striking feature. A survey made in the mid-sixties, covering five hundred directors, found that these men spent over twenty hours a week in meetings and discussions, and only 7 percent of this time was devoted to discussing the actual development of production. There must really be something radically wrong when directors of Czechoslovak enterprises spend eight hours a week on correspondence, four and a half hours on drawing up reports and statements, and almost two and a half hours in telephone conversations, while the preparation and organization of work consumes four hours and study occupies a mere six hours a week. (2)

If we were to look for some parallel between Czechoslovakia

and experience in the West, we might perhaps discover it in the
history of the Ford Motor Company, which found itself on the
verge of collapse thanks only to the inappropriate management
practiced by Henry Ford. Only when he died and Henry Ford II
took over was there a sharp change for the better; and improvement did not even stem from new techniques, but from the work
of new, young and able people brought into management. Peter
F. Drucker had this to say about the old man's methods: "Fundamental to Henry Ford's misrule was a systematic, deliberate
and conscious attempt to run the billion-dollar business without
managers. The secret police that spied on all Ford executives
served to inform Henry Ford of any attempt on the part of one
of his executives to make a decision. When they seemed to acquire managerial authority or responsibility of their own, they
were generally fired." (3)

One really has the feeling that Drucker is talking about recent practice in Czechoslovakia. Indeed, it is hard to resist
substituting for Ford the names of some of the people who
deigned to step down only after January 5, 1968. And at this
point I would like to return to the subject of the Czechoslovak
economy because it seems to me that in our socialist world the
economic and political spheres are linked vessels. The level in
the one has to adjust to the level in the other. I believe, for instance, that no one would have been able to enforce the directive method of economic management in the Soviet Union at the
beginning of the twenties if democratic principles of political
life had been fully operative. And, on the other hand, I would
be unable to write so freely about the complicated problems of
our economy under a directive system of management. The
reason why the old-guard politicians in Czechoslovakia were
compelled to relinquish their positions was not just that quite
a few members of our Communist Party's Central Committee
managed to overstep the limits of their own courage, but also
because these old hands had suffered a disastrous defeat in the
economic field.

The fact is that in our part of the world economics and politics are reflected in the same social mirror. There could be

no system of economic hierarchy if the same principles were not operative in the political set-up. The situation where the market failed to confront the plan as an accepted contender was simply a replica of the political system where public opinion could not oppose the all-powerful central authority. Enterprises were unable to operate as independent economic units when group interests could not even make headway in the political sphere. Indeed, the deadening of business enterprise went hand in hand with the overall political lethargy and the decline of the status of the citizen all along the line.

But we can also transform these linked vessels. If we manage to make radical changes in the economic field, we can create a system of guarantees that will be bound to affect life in the political sphere as well. At the moment we want to break up the entire directive machine that has been managing our economic life with such a notable lack of success. The point is not merely that new ideas should be carried out by new people and new institutions, because if we really succeed in breaking up the bureaucratic colossus and in cutting down the economic ministries to the very minimum, there will be an end to the everlasting dictation that has blocked all attempts to revive the market. Then, if the central plan is subjected to the ever-present corrective of the market as its contender, we must expect to find public opinion exerting a constant pressure on central policies in the political sphere, too. Thus, the economic sphere may in itself provide one of the surest guarantees of democratic progress in Czechoslovakia.

The cornerstone of such guarantees on the economic side could, first of all, be workers' councils in the enterprises. We have heard many doubts expressed about this idea. Some fear, for instance, that such councils might be inclined to choose accommodating managing directors, that they might not be able to ensure competent management selection. Yet if the central institutions have managed for decades by appointing managerial personnel at random, without regard for enterprise needs, why should we not trust workers' councils to be at least equally qualified to do the job? In any case, if the state is losing the function that gave it the inalienable right to decide the fate of any economic unit, who else but the workers' councils should assume the responsibility for appointing directors? After all, the employees of an enterprise bear the immediate consequences of their own undertakings, which includes the results of good or bad decisions made by their managers. And while officials drawing fixed salaries have, until recently, handled millions in funds with almost no risk to themselves, why should not the people who actually feel the impact of financial results be able at least to share in decision-making?

The idea, then, is to have a type of democratic workers' self-administration that would restrict bureaucratic decision-making as much as possible. Equally it should be an organization involving the most modern management methods and employing the services of highly trained personnel. That is what we have in mind in setting up workers' councils in the enterprises and the economic councils, with various commissions of experts, at the local and federal government levels.

This socialist self-administration system is still in preparation and all of its links are not at an equally advanced stage. Therefore we cannot speak in as practical terms of some as of others. While, for example, it has already been decided to set up workers' councils in the enterprises, discussions on the system to be established at the national level are still in their initial stages.

One cannot exclude the possibility that the workers' councils may prove to be the seed of a new self-governing model for the entire country. Producers' groups may one day come to be associated in one chamber of Parliament, thereby enabling them to be, so to speak, participants in dealing with matters that are of immediate concern to them. If the councils then provide a sure safeguard against the dictates of central power in the economy, this may, indeed will, be one of the foremost guarantees that in politics, too, there will never be a recurrence of the old high-handed methods and the supreme rule of a handful of the mighty.

Admittedly, there may be occasions when workers' councils

will choose managing directors who will be willing to pursue an allegedly popular policy and not make great demands on their personnel. Nor can one exclude the possibility that some councils may force directors to put wage growth before investment expenditures. I would like to believe that they will not show such shortsightedness. But in any case, if the councils should go all out for short-term gains, they will soon feel the consequences of their mistakes. Experience will teach them that to choose a "popular" director or to make unjustified wage claims does not pay. The weak manager will not be equal to the job of guiding an enterprise in the complex conditions of the Czechoslovak economy, and a momentary pressure on wages could tie up the sources of growth in living standards for some years ahead.

The great majority of workers' representatives are undoubtedly aware of all these pitfalls. And I really see no reason why we should suspect them in particular of being unable to guarantee a more objective and stricter selection of personnel than we have had under the system of administrative, bureaucratic decision-making. Equally, there is no reason to fear that the authority of a managing director would suffer under the control of a workers' council. A capable, just, but uncompromising and exacting executive, with a good approach to people, will be all the more respected, especially when the employees are aware of his good qualities. Actually there are few such managers, although we all know some, and we shall need more and more of them. Quite soon we shall be faced with a shortage, as in every advanced industrial country.

The enterprise managers, for their part, stand to gain as regards security of tenure. As long as they make no serious mistakes in their economic decisions and commit no grave political offenses, they will be sure of their positions for some years — indeed, they will have legal safeguards. Up to now these men have not known the day or the hour when they might be shown the door; they were entirely dependent on the will of authorities whose word could not be challenged.

Nor is there any need to fear a restriction of management

authority. The terminology itself indicates that "self-administration" means administering the affairs of an enterprise, while
the management will have to manage or direct. The point at
which administration of affairs ends and management starts
will be given legal definition.

At the moment it is difficult to foresee the outcome. We simply know that 1968 has presented Czechoslovakia once again
with a historic opportunity to build a socialist social order
modeled according to her own experience and conditions. We
know, too, that radical changes in economic management can
provide one of the guarantees that this time we shall not let the
opportunity slip.

CHAPTER 6

OUR PROSPECTS

OUR PROSPECTS

Before I had reached this sixth and last talk in the television series, letters were piling up on my desk. They contained fresh arguments, personal experiences, and also offers of help. Indeed, almost everyone who responded in writing to my five preceding talks has offered help. And in reading through this abundant correspondence I realized that for many Czechoslovak citizens this had been their first insight into the nature and abnormality of our economy. In a way I was glad that the none-too-happy picture had not left, and could not leave, viewers indifferent. There remained the last talk, which was to provide an answer to the question posed in the majority of the letters, and which I have also heard at many meetings and conferences. Have we any hope of throwing off the legacy of the past? What are our prospects? We will help, but tell us how long we shall have to tighten our belts.

The answer is not as simple as it might seem. And if I am to try to give it in as comprehensible a form as possible, I shall have to lay myself open to criticism from my fellow economists that I am simplifying the subject. But I am anxious to be understood by a wide public, including people who are encountering many economic problems for the first time in a broader setting. And if I am to put my personal impression in a few words, I am bound to say that the Czechoslovak situation is not so disastrous that we need to resign ourselves to apathy and pessimism. On the other hand, we should not let ourselves be lulled by the rosy optimism that the old-guard politicians tried to implant in the minds of the working people as things grew more and more difficult.

Metaphorically speaking, Czechoslovakia has reached a turning point in her history — not just in the political sense, but also in economic terms. As I said some time ago in Pilsen, we have a good chance of achieving a radical improvement in our present situation, but on the other hand we cannot exclude the possibility of continued stagnation. Indeed, if we go on paying out wages for goods that end up among the stocks of unsalable items, if we expend billions on investment projects that take an interminable time to complete and show a minimal end effect, things may take a decided turn for the worse. The point is that outlays on wages in such cases are not covered by goods and therefore threaten to turn the present creeping inflation into a runaway inflation.

Obviously no one wants that, just as no sensible person can accept the idea that we should so frivolously depreciate the value of our wages and private savings.

My main reason for speaking of this is to point out that the solution does not lie in an unbalanced budget, nor in big demands for fresh investment funds and perhaps claims on wages that are not backed by the real values of salable goods.

Presumably we can all agree that at the fateful crossroads of this and coming years we shall have to choose a second, more hopeful alternative. This alternative promises that within a mere five to seven years the Czechoslovak crown could become convertible, thereby regaining its good name and its proper place in the world of commerce. In this case we should be able to build up a reserve of so-called hard currencies in a relatively short time. Czechoslovak citizens would then be able to exchange their money normally for foreign currency, and they would no longer be put in the position of poor relations when traveling to the West.

Yet this vision has its other side: if we are to reach such a state of affairs within five to seven years, our goods will also have to be exchangeable by then. Our manufactures will have to be really competitive in quality and price; Czechoslovak goods, which no one in the West is actually waiting for, will have to be sufficiently attractive.

We have all experienced three five-year plans and we are now carrying out the fourth, sometimes with greater, more often with less success. Now a new and far more hopeful five-year prospect has been opened up and there is no reason to think that we shall have to tighten our belts all that time or, to put it bluntly, flay the skin off each other. What we must do is simply to work honestly and to learn the art of sound business management, an art which for the most part we know about today solely from the specialist literature. If we fail to learn, there will be no regular flow of dollars and other freely exchangeable currencies to our reserve and the vision of the convertible crown will also fade.

What, then, are the primary requirements if we are to succeed in all this? Three hundred years ago John Amos Comenius wrote that whoever truly wants to achieve something must fulfill three fundamental conditions: he must want to, be able to, and know how. I have no doubt that most of us want to, for who can enjoy working on things that end up among stocks of unsalable goods or are disposed of on the market at a frightful loss? And who in this land of ours, where everyone has realized how much our lives depend on economic prosperity, can fail to wish that we should take our place among the wealthy nations?

The second condition — to be able to — has been finally fulfilled by the Czechoslovak Spring, which this year has started in January. A mere six months have seen formerly unassailable gods and institutions being forced to step down from the Olympus of bureaucratic management. But this must go on. If the market economy is to continue growing, all superfluous departmental institutions of central industrial management will have to be dismantled and the enterprise sphere will have to be genuinely separated from the state administration. Then perhaps we shall see an end to the old practice whereby the overgrown administrative apparatus sledgehammered any enterprising undertakings just to prove its right to exist.

There remains the second half of the question: What body should replace the bureaucratic structure ? Should it be, as I believe, a strong economic council which, instead of issuing the usual commands, orders and resolutions, would regulate our economic life primarily by creating a healthy climate for our enterprises and by setting the economic rules of the game ? Then, at last, enterprises would have to get used to the unfamiliar feeling that their behavior on the socialist market will not be prescribed by anyone at the top, that they will simply have to steer their own course along the route marked out by credit, price, wage, and other conditions.

This necessarily implies giving Czechoslovak enterprises some certainty about the chief guideposts for their future, so that they will know what kinds of taxes they will have to pay and, at least approximately, at what rates, what the bank rate will be, and roughly what price movements may be expected. There are many more conditions, and they will be stated before the year is out in the government's economic guidelines. One must remember, however, that there can never be any absolute certainty. The state can, after all, only guarantee the factors over which it has complete control.

Therefore, in our difficult situation, with all its contradictions, successful performance will also depend upon the way in which enterprises manage to foresee the probable development of market and competitive factors within the limits set by the state. Moreover, they will have to get used to the idea that not even a socialist enterprise can escape some measure of business risk. But it will be easier to predict the movements of economic factors than to speculate about the obscure moods, subjective ideas, and sudden changes of mind of the rulers on whose modest economic abilities the country has had to rely for so many years.

The government's economic guidelines for 1969, which for all practical purposes are now complete, represent the first definite economic measure on the part of the new Cabinet. They map out the main points of the course to be followed by the economy in the immediate future. They also open the hard

fight that has to be fought over the entire front of the Czechoslovak economy if we are to overcome the gravitational pull of
past years.

The first concern is to work for a balanced budget, if not for
a budget surplus. And if the consumer is not to bear the brunt
of growing demands and the whole burden of our legacy from
the past, the government will have to look for additional resources in the enterprises. To cover essential outlays, the
state treasury will simply have to draw on industrial concerns,
where primary incomes are formed. On the other hand, we can
never permit a return to the old practice of confiscating enterprise financial resources to the last crown and heller. If we
did that, we would have to eliminate the whole central idea of
industrial initiative from our program. And our prime concern
is, after all, to replace the system of obedience and command
by a model that relies on human interest and the spirit of enterprise.

Furthermore, it is imperative that we close all the openings
through which funds not backed by goods have been finding their
way into the economy, thereby involving the grave danger of an
inflationary spiral. Over one hundred billion sunk in capital-
under-construction and two hundred billion lying in the warehouses (largely as unsalable goods) offer a sufficiently serious
threat and lesson for the future. Therefore the government
guidelines for 1969 envisage a reduction in capital-under-
construction and a slowdown in the overly rapid growth rate of
investment activity. Nevertheless we shall, of course, carefully consider and select the progressive projects that are essential for our effort to modernize and make big structural
changes. But the limit of new construction will have to be set
lower than in the past.

In addition, the government will close the channels through
which national income has been seeping away. One really cannot stand by with folded arms as goods manufactured at enormous cost escape to the less demanding markets, often at the
price of accepting credit conditions that Czechoslovakia simply
cannot manage in her present position. What is more, our

economic instruments will have to prevent a substantial part
of our national income from being swallowed up in warehouse
stocks. By next year our firms will have smaller financial resources at their disposal than they have today, so not even their
reserve funds will be available to finance output that would pile
up instead of reaching the market. Credit limits will put a stop
to any tendencies for stocks to grow at the expense of bank
credit. Therefore, we are at last approaching the day when
even in Czechoslovakia an accumulation of unsalable goods will
play the same role as in any healthy economy — it will literally
compel enterprises to revise their production programs and to
react more flexibly to market demand.

Finally, the government has no intention of overlooking the
way in which the less successful concerns are vegetating in the
shelter of protectionist policies. Of course, such policies are
practiced everywhere to a greater or lesser extent. There has
to be some protection for industrial branches, or concerns, that
are just going into operation and are in danger of being crushed
by sharp competition before they can achieve what is expected
of them. The Czechoslovak government, too, has to pursue such
policies towards its young, progressive branches. But we shall
have to reconcile ourselves to the fact that doping prescribed
by the treasury cannot, as hitherto, give lasting protection to
producers who operate at a loss. This practice will have to be
revised, both in relation to firms producing for the home
market and to those ineffective exporters who have been relying on the state and the prospering enterprises to meet
their losses. The government envisages that, in the first
place, the present system of grants and tax relief will be
curtailed to the extent that selling clearly ineffective goods
on foreign markets is checked. Insofar as such products
show a tendency to make their way to the less demanding markets, the unprofitable plants producing them will be given subsidies only in exceptional cases where the transactions may
seem essential for reasons of trade policy. But this will just
be the exception that proves the rule. On the other hand, the
government is determined to leave some share of extra profits

to those producers who perform effectively. Such firms will
also be encouraged by credit and investment policies to build
up their production potentials.

We shall then have laid the groundwork that will enable the
Czechoslovak economy to begin, at last, to open up to the world
and to offer competitive goods. The way will also have been
opened to making deeper structural changes throughout the
economy. The government has decided to provide broad opportunities primarily to the most progressive branches. Nonpro-
duction investment — transport and communications, housing,
health, services, education and science — will have priority
over production investment, and in the sphere of production
there will be greater opportunities for the highly effective,
modern branches that symbolize the present century and have
suffered years of neglect.

Furthermore, the government guidelines for 1969 envisage a
further development of the market. This again implies that
prices, which were frozen under the old political and economic
system, will be subjected to a gradual thaw. I can well imagine
that not everyone will greet this step with enthusiasm, and especially that it will not be viewed with great confidence, but it
has to be remembered that price freezing has never yet solved
any economic problem. For years there has been talk in Czechoslovakia about firm prices being a sign of stability, and yet
there were processes at work deep below this apparently calm
surface that have seriously disturbed our economic life.

Anyone who has had even a passing acquaintance with the subject of prices in this country will agree that our economists are
right in saying that value relations have been distorted beyond
all recognition. We sometimes pay exorbitant taxes on many
products simply because someone at the center has fixed them
that way quite arbitrarily. For instance, it has been noted in
the press that polyester fabric that sells for 132 crowns has a
wholesale price no higher than 30.11 crowns. Rude pravo has
stated that an electric cooker type ES 133, priced wholesale at
615 crowns sells retail for 2,700 crowns. It is no wonder that
our consumption is often restricted by high prices, although we

may have sufficient domestic raw materials and adequate production capacities for the articles concerned. On the other hand, we can buy some products in the shops at amazingly low prices. When the state is keeping the prices down by means of subsidies there is no hope of preventing the goods from being sold out. Yet with the best will in the world the producer is unable to turn out more, even when we ignore the shortages of raw materials from abroad.

This means that we shall have to proceed by degrees to eliminate discrepancies in the turnover tax. Some prices will have to drop sharply, while others will inevitably have to go up. The change will not be sudden, but it will have to be made if we want to establish market relations, to get our goods exchangeable on foreign markets, and if our aim is to have the value relations of the world market reflected in the Czechoslovak economy. We cannot allow the domestic consumer to suffer the full impact, but while keeping a constant check on movements in price levels, we shall have to see to it that the present freezing of price absurdities is gradually ended. I would like to remind anyone who is afraid of price movements that up to the moment when the new team took over the reins of government, the consumer was groping around between hidden price rises and a shortage of many types of consumer and nonconsumer goods. The present government is trying to correct this abnormal state of the market with the least possible impact on the life of the people. It will maintain a constant watch on price indexes and make certain that growth in nominal incomes is sufficient to keep real incomes moving upward. Incidentally, the guidelines for next year envisage a 9 percent growth in personal consumption, which would be an unprecedented rate for this factor. The government also intends to promote the consumer and food industries, the output of building materials, and housing construction — primarily by tax relief, preferential credit terms, and other economic measures. Our plan for 460,000 dwellings by 1970, and also the outlook on the consumer market, undoubtedly depend on the implementation of precisely these projects. Moreover, priority will be given in foreign trade transactions

to importing the raw materials needed by our consumer industries. We also envisage a rise in imports of automobiles from
the capitalist world and, on the other hand, a cut in exports of
some consumer goods manufactured by the engineering industry. Here, too, automobiles are on the list. First and foremost,
however, the government's aim is to stop the practice of administrative intervention, with its strict commands and futile re-
strictions. For example, the draft guidelines propose abolishing the rigid tying of productivity growth to wages. That absurd
equation, as we have seen in the foregoing chapters, did not
bring about any saving of raw materials or labor; on the contrary, it resulted in wanton squandering.

If we really succeed in meeting the basic requirements of
this program, then I am quite confident that our enterprises,
or at least the majority of them, will fulfill the third condition
of which I have spoken. That is to say, they will, in Comenius's
words, know how. Indeed, they will have to know how if they
want to maintain their right to exist and are to stand up credit-
ably to the growing pressure of foreign markets.

Although a few swallows don't make a summer, the first
signs of an emerging spirit of enterprise are to be seen.

One example will serve to illustrate the trend. The Decin
Engineering Works recently broke its connection with the group
under which it had been operating and started to look around
for more useful partners. The reason was simple — its high-
lift trucks had gained quite a good reputation abroad. Its order book would keep it busy for two to three years ahead
and there was little hope of getting state investment resources
to expand its capacity. And so offers to cooperate came from
factories interested in taking a share in this highly attractive
program. The result is that several firms are giving up less
profitable production lines to help the Decin Engineering Works
in the job of nearly trebling its capacity by 1970, and almost
no demands are being made on state investment funds. Naturally we shall hope for many more well-considered projects of
this kind in the near future.

Moreover, Czechoslovak enterprises should not be shy of

cooperating with firms abroad, especially since many French, British, Belgian, Austrian and West German concerns are keenly interested in such cooperation. This is true not because they might be trying to engage in "capitalist diversion," but because they are looking to a hinterland of European industry for support in countering strong American competition. It is up to Czechoslovak works to find such opportunities without, of course, letting themselves be dominated by their Western partners. Their aim should be to take advantage of offers to cooperate in order to modernize plant and introduce new and more effective production and, in addition, to penetrate, with the help of the Western partner, markets that our country either abandoned of its own accord or that have been closed to us over the past twenty years. In short, given her modest size, Czechoslovakia must establish footholds for her trade wherever the opportunity arises. That can be said to be an almost iron law governing our future course.

Simultaneously, the pressure of sophisticated markets impels all branches of Czechoslovak industry to adapt production programs to demand at home and abroad, to manufacture at competitive costs, and to turn out products that are a match at least for the average, but preferably for the top-quality, products offered by our competitors. Such flexibility is really imperative for survival. As I have said, the public treasury cannot continue indefinitely providing a high barrier of subsidies to protect enterprises that show no promise of earning enough even to cover raw materials and wages. And we can hardly ask the progressive, resourceful firms to provide permanent support from their funds to the backward, less successful, and unadaptable.

Here we have come up against one of the most tricky questions of the day — a problem well known to the old political leadership, but which, as in so many other cases, it refused to tackle. Rather than do anything unpopular, it preferred to do nothing. That, incidentally, is why I think the blame for errors of the past rests with the politicians and not with the experts involved in them. For years the leaders clung to the institutions

that matched the old type of management and to their system
of personnel selection, while anxiously avoiding any step that
might, even for a moment, prove unpopular. While thundering
their opposition to any price raising, they were equally persis-
tent in maintaining the old system of protecting backwardness
and ineffectiveness in industry. It was really political weakness
that underlay the failure to do anything at all.

Yet we cannot afford to delay, even though there are bound to
be many misunderstandings and perhaps some short-term conflicts as well. The fact is that many people still see this fundamental question from the standpoint of the prewar capitalist
Republic with its mass unemployment. But this is a false approach, if only because the government of a socialist country
is hardly likely to allow the employees of closed plants to sink
into poverty. The treasury will not be willing to subsidize un-
successful concerns, but it will give moral and financial support to the man who is looking for a new job and perhaps would
be prepared to go into an entirely new trade or profession. He
will have to be given compensation for loss of earnings and, of
course, the costs of prompt retraining will be borne by public
funds. There will be circumstances in which he should be offered really generous compensation. After all, the old system
gave the employee no opportunity to influence the production
program of his factory, nor could he say anything about investment policies, so we cannot shift the consequences on to his
shoulders. No advanced industrial country has escaped these
problems, and we will be no exception. If some Western countries have produced programs for minimizing the social impact, it would be a disgrace if a socialist system failed to provide at least equally good care for its people.

I had all this in mind when I said at a government press con-
ference two months ago that we do not envisage unemployment
but that we cannot exclude the possibility that pockets of short-
term unemployment will appear while new job openings are being found and redundant workers are being retrained. This answer evoked a response from Mr. Oldrich Haban of Brno in the
weekly Reportér. He reminded me that the Constitution of our

Republic guarantees the right to work, and he added that anyone not acting according to this constitutional article should be ex-communicated from the Communist Party.

To my mind this response was a bit exaggerated. After all, the right to work does not imply the right to be employed exclusively in one branch of industry, in a given job or a single profession. Like it or not, any country's economy has to adjust to technological changes and the inescapable demands of the times. Were this not the case, then humanity would never have managed to part with flint-making, the Bronze and Iron Ages, and would never have reached the threshold of the age of macro-molecular chemistry, the chemistry of synthetic materials.

If, today, people such as engineers and doctors find that they have to supplement their training constantly, if in effect they go through study material equivalent to another university course every ten years, I see no reason why the rank-and-file worker in industry should not be able to improve his skill — especially when he can do so at state expense and with the prospect of higher earnings. Five years ago a ladder of job demand was constructed for modern American industry; top places were occupied by computer staff, laboratory personnel, engineers, secretaries, foremen, natural scientists, and skilled craftsmen, while openings for stokers, farm laborers and semi-skilled workers declined. A similar table for Soviet industry shows greatly increased interest in teamsters over pick-and-shovel workers, and top demand is for job-setters and maintenance men, combine-harvester operators, doctors, foremen, laboratory staff, and radiotelegraphists. If living standards are to be promoted, Czechoslovakia cannot afford to go on marking time either. The closure of only 81 branch establishments of national enterprises in 1967 is nothing to boast of; indeed, this figure is below that of 1966, when there were 204 closures. (1)

In many cases, of course, it is perfectly possible to avoid closures by switching production programs in time. For example, the plant used for ore-refining at Ejpovice has now found a new and more useful program. This, too, is a way of scrapping outdated production. Uncompetitive enterprises can also make contracts with the government, stating a time limit within which they intended to catch up with foriegn competitors, and if their prospects seem realistic, they can rely on state aid.

At this point I should like to say something on the subject of a foreign loan. My own view is that a long-term loan of 300 to 500 million dollars could (as long as there were no political strings attached to it) accelerate technological reconstruction and modernization in our industrial enterprises. This is especially true in the sectors where Czechoslovakia can take pride in an excellent tradition. And a loan would help to get us over the period when we would be speeding up the closure of ineffective plant. Quite simply, we would win a much-needed breathing space and be able to stop hunting for goods to export to hard currency areas at any price, and whatever the losses, just because our currency reserves were inadequate. One need hardly point out that the incredible losses on such transactions are met by the public treasury out of funds provided by all of us, enterprises and private citizens, through the taxes we pay. These are the reasons why the government is engaging in certain discussions concerning a loan, bearing in mind the need for an arrangement that will be politically and economically most advantageous for our country. However, we can help ourselves in many respects from our own resources. For instance, we can decide at last, after nearly two years of compromising, to adopt the principles of the new management system, and to adopt it to the full extent. Instead of merely playing at using the market, the market economy and the mechanism of supply and demand should become the real driving force of our undertakings. Only then will we be able to envisage a shift to a consumers' market. Meanwhile, as we all know very well, we are at the mercy of the producer, who only too often relies on our having to buy anything available because goods in the required assortments and quality have simply not been in the shops for years.

The competitive mechanism will help, too — in production and in commerce. Therefore I believe that cooperative businesses and factory sales outlets should increasingly appear on

the market. And since there are bound to be gaps in any industrial economy, I see no reason why groups of, say, ten or so
enterprising citizens should not be able to form a cooperative,
especially if they can cater to some unfulfilled need in consumption and are able to find a place to work. I even think that the
state should help such enterprising people by providing cheap
credit, by keeping taxation at a tolerable level, and by offering
other advantages.

We all know quite well that a craftsman working with his family and no more than one or two apprentices really cannot be a
danger to socialism. In the German Democratic Republic much
bigger private undertakings have done no harm to the socialist
system, and therefore we should at least make use of the people who have retained the flair for craftsmanship traditional
among the Czechs. They are badly needed in the service sector, where the range of facilities available is almost at the level
of a developing country. And if we encourage this spirit of enterprise we may encourage people who have faith in their own
hands not to hang on until some chronically unprofitable concern closes down.

Moreover, even small economic units, if they are enterprising, may be able to help accelerate the solution of the very difficult problem of Czechoslovakia's housing program. The Economic Council has already considered some possibilities. As
regards the price preferences for housing construction compared with industrial investment, which the Council is working
on, I cannot speak in detail at this stage.

Talks are also in progress with respect to the Yugoslav contribution to building ten to twenty thousand homes, and we are
seeking every possible way of expanding production capacities
in the building industry. The Economic Council also expects
cooperatives to lend a hand. Why should cooperative farms not
use their production and transport resources to help in construction work? Old quarries could be opened up, and old brick-
works too, perhaps with financial support from local authorities
or the government. Perhaps industrial enterprises will decide
to make some efforts in this direction, encouraged by the fact

that the Economic Council is considering tax relief to firms
that invest part of their resources in housing for their employees and manage to utilize their own construction facilities and
some building materials for this purpose.

In short, there are plenty of ways and means available. And
this does not apply to housing alone. Henceforth no enterprise
or cooperative can expect to receive precise orders and advice
from the top. They will have to rely on their own initiative and
imagination to find suitable outlets for their work.

And this brings us to the nub of the problem. There can be
no doubt that a socialist economy needs a strong and skilled
center of management. But this alone will yield nothing if the
efforts expended fail to meet with a proper response, indeed
with support, in the form of flexible socialist enterprise in the
true interests of society as a whole.

This is all the more vital at a time when Czechoslovakia
finds herself at the divide between two epochs, at a time when
we are equally close to unforeseen prosperity and to narrowing
the big gap dividing us from the Western world as we are to advancing stagnation and the perils of inflation. If we can rely on
the interest expressed by viewers in their letters, and if this
interest materializes in deeds, then we have nothing to fear.
Quite the contrary.

There is a great deal of work confronting us: remodeling the
system of management, making radical changes in the industrial structure, establishing new types of organization, changing over to a federal type of government. But if the widespread
initiative among our two nations, the Czechs and Slovaks, is
maintained, if we regain confidence in our not inconsiderable
abilities and brace ourselves to throw off the dead weight of
the past as well, then we may be able within a few years to record some tangible results of our liberated endeavor.

INTRODUCTION TO AMERICAN EDITION

1) A. Novotný, Projevy, Vol. 1 (1954-56 speeches), Publishing House of Political Literature (NPL), Prague, 1964, pp. 137-138.

2) Novotný, ibid., Vol. 3 (1962-64), NPL, Prague, 1964, p. 180.

3) Ibid., p. 183.

4) Gustav Husák, speaking in Moravia, as reported in Rude pravo, August 30, 1971.

5) "They chose a hazardous course, they wanted to break up, to subvert, our society, to tear it away from the socialist camp, and so they have to bear certain consequences — although compared with the harm they have caused these are really negligible and very mild" (G. Husák, Rude pravo, August 30, 1971).

6) Novotný's address to the 10th Congress of the CPC, in Rude pravo, June 12, 1954. In Novotný's "Collected Works," published in 1964, the whole of the attack on the Husák group has been omitted from the speech (Projevy, Vols. 1, 2, 3 [1954-64]; see, in particular, Vol. 1, p. 98).

CHAPTER 1

1) Analýza příčin vývojových tendencí o stavu čs. národního hospodářství (Analysis of the Causes of Development Trends in

the Czechoslovak Economy), Ministry of Economic Planning, Prague, 1968. (Referred to henceforth as Analysis of Causes.)

2) Ibid.

3) V. I. Lenin, Left-Wing Communism, An Infantile Disorder, in Selected Works, Vol. 3, Moscow, 1967, pp. 350, 356.

4) Dvacet let rozvoje ČSSR (Twenty Years in the Development of the CSSR), Prague, 1965, p. 33. (Henceforth: Twenty Years.)

5) Analysis of Causes.

6) Ibid.

7) Ibid.

8) Ibid.

9) Twenty Years, p. 82.

10) Calculated by Dr. Souček.

11) Study by the Ministry of Finance, in Hospodářské noviny, 1968, No. 25.

12) S. Rudik, My a oni — srovnávací studie (We and They — A Comparative Study), Prague, 1966. (Henceforth: We and They.)

13) Hospodářské noviny, 1966, No. 18.

14) Study and calculations by Karol Černý.

15) Report by the Ministry of Finance, in Hospodářské noviny, 1968, No. 26.

16) Study and calculations by Karol Černý.

CHAPTER 2

1) Twenty Years, p. 75 (data for 1963).

2) Analysis of Causes.

3) We and They (data for 1961).

4) Ibid. (data for 1964).

5) Ibid.

6) Radovan Richta, Civilization at the Crossroads, Prague-New York, 1969, p. 313.

7) Hospodářské noviny, 1966, Nos. 19, 32.

8) L. Říha, Ekonomická efektivnost vědeckotechnického pokroku (Economic Effectiveness of Scientific and Technological

Progress), Prague, 1965, pp. 122-132.

9) Calculations by Dr. V. Nachtigal; for dollar/Czech crown conversion, an exchange rate of 1:14 was used.

10) Analysis of Causes.

11) Ibid.

12) Ibid.

13) Čísla pro každého (Figures for Everyone), Prague, 1967, p. 136.

14) Analysis of Causes.

15) Ibid.

16) Ibid.

17) Ibid.

18) Ibid.

19) Ibid.

CHAPTER 3

1) Ibid.

2) Calculations by Stanislav Lupták, Reportér (Prague), 1967, No. 4, pp. 12-13.

3) Engineer Josef Hubálek, Packaging Institute, Prague.

4) Hospodářské noviny, 1966, No. 18.

5) Analysis of Causes.

6) A survey of reproduction costs of selected items of Czechoslovak export (Ministry of Foreign Trade paper, 1967).

7) Analysis of Causes.

8) Information by Minister of Foreign Trade, V. Valeš, in Hospodářské noviny, 1968, No. 26.

9) Data for 1936, 1937, 1947 and 1949 at 1963 prices; for 1961, 1963 and 1966 at current prices.

10) For Germany the year is 1936, for Czechoslovakia — 1937.

11) For Germany — 1949, Czechoslovakia — 1947.

12) Statistická ročenka 1966, pp. 681-684.

13) Information by the Minister of Foreign Trade, V. Valeš.

CHAPTER 4

1) Srovnávací studie o životni úrovní v ČSSR, NSR a Rakousku (Comparison of Living Standards in Czechoslovakia, West Germany and Austria), Prague, 1967, pp. 18-26.

2) Ibid., p. 27.

3) Analysis of Causes.

4) Ibid.

5) Ibid.

6) Obtained by conversion using Czechoslovak price statistics, data from the paper Scale, and the price list of the Neckermann department store.

7) Analysis of Causes.

8) Hospodářské noviny, 1968, No. 23.

9) Ibid.

10) Comparison of Living Standards, pp. 37-42.

11) Figures for Everyone, p. 180.

12) Analysis of Causes.

13) We and They.

14) Analysis of Causes.

15) Ibid.

16) Report by Minister of Health, Dr. Vlcek.

17) Hospodářské noviny, 1966, No. 21.

18) A Šteker, in Hospodářské noviny, 1966, No. 28.

19) Ibid.

20) Hospodářské noviny, 1966, No. 21.

21) Hospodářské noviny, 1968, No. 28.

22) Ibid.

23) Official report.

24) Official report.

25) Consultation with members of the staff of the State Office of Statistics.

26) Analysis of Causes.

27) Data from official statistics and the comparative study We and They.

28) Analysis of Causes.

29) We and They.

30) Hospodářské noviny, 1966, No. 21.

31) Analysis of Causes.

32) Source material for Analysis of Causes.

CHAPTER 5

1) Information from the foreign press.

2) We and They.

3) Peter F. Drucker, The Practice of Management, New York and Evanston, Harper & Row, 1954, p. 114.

CHAPTER 6

1) Analysis of Causes.

INDEX

Agriculture, 62 ff.
Alienation, 20, 101
Anti-Semitism, 17

Bilak, V., 15
Bureaucracy, 19, 20, 57, 62
  bureaucratic machine, 4,
    11-12, 44, 101
  bureaucratic regime, 7, 19,
    28, 116

Capitalism, state, 20
Censorship, 6, 8, 22, 31
Centralistic system, 8, 27 ff.,
  101, 115
COMECON, 42-43
Comenius, 115, 121
Communists, orthodox, 26 ff.
Communist Party of Czecho-
  slovakia, 17
  antireform campaign, 26
  party machine, 18-19
  power monopoly, 7-8
Communist Party of the Soviet
  Union, 44

Competition, 78-79, 80, 125
  ability to compete, 50, 57,
    74 ff., 100, 115
  pressure on enterprises,
    5, 34, 116
Consumer goods, 86-87
Czechoslovak economy
  development, 41 ff., 55 ff.,
    100
  lag behind capitalist coun-
    tries, 6, 26
  reasons for extensive de-
    velopment, 42
  transition to centralized
    planning, 4, 100

Democracy, 7, 19, 106 ff.
  tradition in Czechoslo-
    vakia, 17
Drucker, P. F., 105
Dubček, A., 7

Economic reform, 7, 11 ff.,
  30, 45, 106
  fight against, 12 ff., 30

135

Economists, 3-4, 6, 21, 44
   dogmatic approach, 31, 46
   economic studies, 6-7, 13,
      30, 45, 94
Economy and politics, 99, 105,
   114, 122
   democratization, 106
   self-management, 7, 18,
      106-07
Elections, 8, 19-20
Enterprises, 5, 11, 13, 32 ff.,
   57, 76 ff., 101
   cooperation with foreign
      firms, 122
   independence, 11-12, 14, 115
   managers, directors, 11,
      102 ff., 108 ff.
Extensive economic growth,
   29, 41 ff., 46 ff., 73
   construction, 49-51
   domestic production, 43,
      49-50
   enterprise behavior, 101
   foreign trade, 43
   investment, 13, 49, 91
   management appointments,
      102
   obsolescence of capital
      assets, 46 ff.
   self-sufficiency, 73-74

Food consumption, 87-88
Ford, Henry, 105
Foreign trade, 43, 71 ff., 118,
   120-22
   abnormality, 76, 77
   balance of payments deficit,

   73-74, 76, 78
   dependence on, 71
   developing countries, 78
   foreign loan, 125
   losses, 10, 61, 74 ff.
   monopoly, 7, 79
   prices, 72-73, 76-77
Frank, J., 44
Frejka, L., 44

Gross National Product, 84 ff.
Gross output indicator, 56-
   57, 60-62

Housing, 51, 89 ff., 120,
   126-27
   rents, 89
Husák, G., 7, 8, 9-10, 11, 12,
   14 ff.
   regime of, 10, 21

Incentives, 50, 59
Indra, A., 15
Industrial structure, 6, 14,
   43, 47-48, 56, 60, 117
Ineffective performance, 47,
   57 ff., 76
   factors of production, 13
Inflation, 78, 114
   anti-inflation policies, 15,
      117
   "controlled," 13
Intensive economic development, 41
Investment, 12, 13, 21, 47 ff.,
   85, 119
   capital-under-construction,

10, 51, 117
construction time, 50-51
effectiveness, 13, 49
expansion, 12, 49
structural change, 14, 52, 119

Labor
employment of women,
92-93
mobilization appeals, 8-9
right to work, 124
working morale, 20, 83
Lenin, V. I., 45-46
Living standard, 8, 12, 21, 32-
33, 83 ff.
consumer durables, 86-87
diet 87-88
economic reform, 120
housing, 51, 89-91
personal consumption, 86 ff.
potential growth, 29
services, 88, 92 ff.

Management
in West, personnel training,
103-04
level of, 62, 66, 83, 101 ff.
Management system, "im-
proved," 45
Market
mechanism, stimuli, 4, 5,
11, 31, 57, 104, 125
need for, 4, 5, 11, 45, 67
planned regulation, 11, 34 ff.
pressure, 11 ff., 21, 122
renewal of, 67, 116, 119 ff.
Model of new economic system,

6-7, 12, 31, 33, 36
Monopoly
in foreign trade, 7, 79
in industry, 4, 7, 11
measures against, 15

National income, 6, 49, 73,
117
National Front, 19
"Normalization" in Czechoslovakia, 8
Novotný, A., 7, 8-9, 10, 11-
12, 14 ff., 25, 35

Personal consumption, 5, 6,
28 ff., 85 ff.
in capitalist countries, 6,
85
Personnel policy, 18, 102-
03, 123
Plan and market, 31 ff.
Planning administration, 13,
15
fighting reform, 12
indicators, 56
methods and law of value,
45
Planning, central, 3, 7, 10,
51, 100
bureaucratic, 4 ff., 21, 48,
56
macroeconomic and dem-
ocratic, 32, 100
Political system, Stalinist,
14, 18-19
Political trials, 4, 15-16, 17
Population, 91-92

Prague Spring, 10, 14, 115
Prices
    fixed, 4, 32, 57, 76-77, 119
    growth, 12, 120
    market, 5, 13, 119-20
    world, 13, 32
Production, costs of, 5, 74
Production incentives, 5, 50,
    59, 77, 100-01, 118
Productivity, 6, 31, 47, 60, 62,
    65-66, 121
Protectionism, 33, 78, 118, 122

Quality of output, 5, 57 ff.,
    72 ff.

Retraining in industry, 35, 124

Schulz, Prof. G., 39 ff.
Socialism, 6, 7, 11, 16, 17, 18,
    27, 48, 126
Soviet domination, 15, 16

Soviet military intervention,
    3, 5, 15, 20
Soviet system, 3, 14
    imposed model, 4, 41, 56
Stalin, J. V., 42, 44
Stocks, accumulation, 51, 66
Supply and demand, 10, 45, 66
Svoboda, L., 15

Technological base, 56, 59 ff.,
    72 ff.
    obsolescence, 10, 21, 32,
        46 ff., 58
    potential, 56, 95, 103
Tertiary sector, 20, 93

Wage movement, 84, 95
    criteria, 57, 60, 62, 121
Wastage of production re-
    sources, 60 ff., 77
Workers' councils, self-
    management, 7, 18, 106 ff.